GOLDEN

TWR's 50-year journey of bringing Jesus to Africa

Hannah Davis and John Lundy

GOLDEN

TWR's 50-year journey of bringing Jesus to Africa

P.O. Box 4232
Kempton Park, South Africa
twr.org/africa

PUBLISHED IN THE UNITED STATES OF AMERICA

Contents

Foreword

Claudia Schmidt

Director of International Ministries, ERF Medien

I LEARNED ABOUT the beginnings of TWR's ministry in Africa mainly from reports of some of my TWR colleagues and from Horst Marquardt's book *My History With ERF: Waiting – Wonders – Waves*. He describes his first encounters with Stephen Boakye-Yiadom, a man you'll read about in the pages of this book, in the following way:

"I want to work for the radio mission in Africa," Stephen said. I had to reply regretfully that TWR had no field of work there (at that time). "And besides," I added, "someone who wants to do radio ministry properly needs theological and journalistic training." Four years later, Stephen was back in my office. "Now I have a theological education, and now I want to go to Africa!" Regretfully, I had to tell him that I still did not know of any plans for a TWR project in Africa. About 14 days later, Bill Mial called on behalf of Dr. Freed and told me: "Listen, we are

*going to set up a transmitter in Swaziland to broadcast to African countries. Don't
you know someone who could help us?"**

Boakye-Yiadom then received some basic journalism training at
ERF facilities in Wetzlar, the city where TWR's German national
partner is based, and a few months later, he was sent to Nairobi to start
a radio ministry in Africa. At this point, Marquardt's report ends. But
God's story with TWR Africa continues.

After Marquardt connected Boakye-Yiadom with TWR founder
Paul Freed and with Dr. Freed's chief lieutenant, Bill Mial, the young
Ghanaian whose motto was "Africa needs Jesus" went on to become
TWR's widely admired international director for his home continent.
I think this little story is a wonderful example of how ERF and TWR,
which have been partners since 1959, have shared a deep concern for
ministry across Africa since the 1950s, when the two media organiza-
tions officially became partners.

Reading the different stories in *GOLDEN: TWR's 50-year Journey of
Bringing Jesus to Africa* about TWR staff makes me realize how great
our God is. Yes, there were huge challenges. But God paved the way.
Miraculously, he provided funds, sometimes even materials and the
right people at the right time. So, in the end, millions of African people
all over the continent could hear the good news of Jesus.

After 50 years we can joyfully look back with a thankful heart and
give all honour and glory to God. It's a moment to pause and cele-
brate. Even the Bible encourages us to do so and remember God's

---

* Horst Marquardt. Meine Geschichte mit dem Evangeliums-Rundfunk: Warten – Wunder –
Wellen. 2002, Hänssler Verlag, Holzgerlingen, S. 171-172.

great deeds – in Exodus 13:14-16, Moses calls for Israelites to commemorate the Lord's rescue of them from slavery in Egypt. This isn't to indulge in the past and forget about the present but to draw strength and courage for the future.

There are new challenges to come, but even greater opportunities lie ahead. As you read the stories of this book, may they fill your heart with joy and confidence, too. God is still at work, and Africa still needs Jesus. It is a wonderful privilege to be part of that story.

CLAUDIA SCHMIDT

Claudia Schmidt (Photo used with permission form ERF.)

After her apprenticeship in business administration, Claudia worked for more than 20 years in international companies. In 2004/2005 she served with Operation Mobilisation in an international team that started a Ministry among Muslim women in Paris/France. After that she studied Theology and Intercultural Studies. In 2013 she received her MA from Columbia International University, German Branch Korntal. In 2012 Claudia joined ERF. Since 2015 she is director of International Ministries at ERF Germany. Since 2023 she is also a member of the TWR International Board. Claudia loves travelling and meeting people from different nations. Since she joined ERF she has been able to visit different countries in Africa. She is fascinated by the beauty and vastness of this continent and its wonderful people.

Acknowledgements

WE WOULD LIKE to express our sincere gratitude to the following individuals without whom GOLDEN would not have come to fruition. Their contributions have made this publication possible.

In 2022, Zeke Hansen, a resident of Corydon, Indiana, embarked on the work of GOLDEN. Zeke, who was completing his summer internship at the TWR Africa office, was a double major in journalism and telecommunications, with a concentration in news, at Ball State University. He transcribed audio and video interviews with long-serving missionaries and staff whose stories are featured in this book, conducting follow-up interviews whenever additional information was needed.

The following summer, we were fortunate to have another intern join TWR Africa. Hannah Davis took the information compiled by

Zeke and conducted further interviews with missionaries and staff, starting the process of writing their TWR stories.

However, there were still countless untold stories of how God had miraculously provided for the ministry, enabling it to not only progress but also experience exponential growth over five decades of broadcasting the Good News of Jesus Christ across the African continent. That's when John Lundy, TWR writer and communication specialist, joined the effort. He dedicated months to conducting additional interviews and writing stories to complete the book.

We extend our gratitude to Jon Hill, writer and editor for TWR, who generously contributed his time and expertise to editing GOLDEN.

Another significant contributor to this publication is Renate Schiele, who serves in the TWR Africa Marketing and Communications Department. Renate not only illustrated and designed the cover and layout of the book but also played a crucial role in guiding the development process of GOLDEN over the past two years. Additionally, she sourced photos and created the illustrations found within the book.

We would like to express our appreciation to the following individuals who graciously made themselves available for interviews, whether in person, online, or over the phone: Larry and Virginia McGuire, Steve and Lorraine Stavropoulos, Andrew Haas (for the video interview with the late Edith Kleynhans), and the children of Evert and Edie Kleynhans, who shared more information about their parents' involvement in the ministry. We would also like to thank Becky Uhden, James and Lyn Burnett, Abdoulaye Sangho, Eberhard Haberkorn, Tobi Pfeiffer, Salema Simelane, Victor Kaonga, Janet Mtali, and Barbara MacDonald (for sharing the late Andrew MacDonald's unpublished memoirs with TWR Africa). Many of these people also provided photos for use in the book.

A special thanks goes to Claudia Schmidt for writing the foreword for GOLDEN.

Above all, we give thanks to God our Father, Jesus our Saviour, and the Holy Spirit for guiding the hearts and minds of everyone involved in the creation of this publication. May God's name be glorified through the testimonies of faithfulness and grace received throughout the five decades of TWR Africa's ministry.

Now to him who is able to do far more abundantly than all that we ask or think, according to the power at work within us, to him be glory in the church and in Christ Jesus throughout all generations, forever and ever. Amen.

Ephesians 3:20-21

Introduction

THE 50 YEARS of TWR in Africa is a story of prayer and passion.

It began much earlier, with Christian groups praying for years that God would bring Christian radio to the southern parts of the continent. One such group met faithfully for 25 years, according to Andrew Mac Donald, a key figure in the story of TWR Africa, in an unpublished memoir.

In the following pages, you will read about the outcomes of their prayers through the experiences of the individuals chosen by God to fulfill his purposes. You will see how God worked through unlikely partnerships and difficult circumstances to do more than they could hope or imagine, to borrow from Ephesians 3:20, extending far beyond the southern regions of Africa.

You'll meet Larry McGuire, who led the team that discovered the Mpangela Ranch site in what was then Swaziland, where TWR transmitters would be located. Due to a misunderstanding, Larry and his wife, Virginia, were not greeted upon their arrival in Johannesburg. In a time before cellphones, and without any change on hand, they found the exact amount needed in the pay phone they used and were able to connect with the TWR office.

Once the site was chosen, the construction process was guided by God's hand, even providing the exact type of sand needed. It was delivered by floodwaters.

You will learn about Stephen Boakye-Yiadom, TWR's first African international director, who summarized his passion with the phrase "Africa needs Jesus!" This passion led him to launch the *Africa Challenge* programme.

Becky Uhden, an American serving for TWR in Europe, was asked in 1993 to spend two years helping set up a Finance Department for the Africa Regional Office. She ended up staying for 23 years.

Andrew MacDonald and his wife, Barbara, who served with TWR in Cape Town and Johannesburg, South Africa, as well as in Manzini, Eswatini, shared the same passion. "Since our first days with TWR, up to the present, we rejoice when a listener finds Jesus Christ as their Saviour through our radio programmes," he wrote.

Longtime TWR engineer James Burnett will take you along as staff members push a wheelbarrow filled with reel-to-reel tapes – state-of-the-art at that time – across a narrow suspension bridge in order to broadcast programmes over the air.

You'll witness the Rev. Abdoulaye Sangho on his knees, attaching egg cartons to a wall to convert a children's bedroom into a recording room for programmes that would be aired by TWR in West Africa.

You'll also witness the remarkable story of two churches that grew under the preaching of TWR's Isac Silvano among Mozambican refugees living in

Swaziland. When conditions improved back home, they dismantled their Swaziland buildings and returned to Mozambique with the materials. Over time, they established 10 new churches.

With passion and prayer, the story continues.

TWR in West Africa is creating *My Story With God*, a programme in which believers from Muslim backgrounds share how they came to have faith in Christ. TWR, along with a partner ministry, is providing Audio Bible Teacher digital devices to prison inmates in eastern and southern Africa. They are also transitioning to solar power at several African locations affected by rolling power cuts.

What Stephen Boakye-Yiadom said is still true today: "Africa needs Jesus!" As the Lord provides, through new and old forms of media, TWR Africa will continue to proclaim the greatest story ever told, because it is a story for everyone.

And we know that for those who love God all things work together for good, for those who are called according to his purpose.

Romans 8:28

1

God's Purpose Accomplished
Despite Lost Telegram

BACK HOME, LARRY and Virginia McGuire had pictured dry heat and cracked ground. Yet while they stood inside the Johannesburg airport, the early August morning outside hovered below freezing and the crisp air instilled a jarring sense of newness and anticipation in the couple.

But as unexpected as the weather was, a greater unforeseeable event waited ahead.

After their wedding in Colorado, Larry and Virginia travelled from church to church every Sunday morning and again on Sunday and Wednesday nights to raise financial support to fly to the Caribbean island of Bonaire, where they would serve at the TWR transmitter site. Larry had already spent nine months in Bonaire as a volunteer before he married Virginia, and his desire to use his engineering skills for the gospel budded there.

During this time of support-raising, Larry worked in construction with his father. It was hard work, and he often went home exhausted. But the Lord's fruit blossomed through their season of diligence, for after nine months of traveling to churches, the young couple were fully funded and ready to head to the mission field.

With hearts ready to help share the good news of the gospel with the people of the Caribbean and Latin America, they flew back to Bonaire, their spirits brimming with joy.

FROM HOT CARIBBEAN TO CHILLY AFRICA

BUT NOW, ABOUT a year since they landed in the Caribbean, they stood in the chilly South African airport, far away from the tropical climate of Bonaire, where August would be one of the hottest times of the year. An hour after midnight, the sunlight had long vanished, and a sense of drowsiness was seeping into the airport. Ready to settle for the night, the passengers had exited the plane, grabbed their baggage and trickled out. Eventually, Larry and Virginia were the last passengers to stand in the airport.

Their flight had been the last one of the day to Johannesburg, so the airport was uncrowded. But their tired eyes couldn't spot a TWR staff member on hand to meet them and take them to their accommodations for the night.

Was their ride late? Had the staff lost track of time or gotten the wrong date?

They didn't have the answer, yet they had a certain peace, a certain knowledge lodged inside them, despite standing alone in a country they'd never stepped foot in before. Even though they had no idea what had caused the airport mishap, they were sure the Lord knew, and he would provide a solution.

He didn't direct them away from Bonaire and to Africa without a purpose.

Soon after they had landed in Bonaire, they heard that there had been a request for volunteers to transfer from Bonaire to South Africa to help build the first TWR transmitter site in Africa. Although they had missed the official announcement, an interest sparked inside them; they had experience living in rough, remote settings, so perhaps the Lord had been preparing them to live in the rural areas of South Africa. Also, they didn't have a place to call home yet in Bonaire and were staying in the home of a missionary who was on furlough. And last of all, they had no children yet, unlike many of the missionary families on Bonaire.

Eagerly, they volunteered, having more than enough funds to support them for the new assignment in Africa. A sense of adventure gripped them as they boarded a flight back home to Colorado and soon caught another one to Monte Carlo, where they stayed a few days with the TWR team before boarding a 10-hour flight to Johannesburg. Filled with bottomless anticipation and curiosity, a blend of excitement permeated with the Lord's peace on their journey.

DID WE MAKE A MISTAKE?

BUT, AS A lonely quietness and emptiness pervaded the Johannesburg airport, doubt could have easily crept in, breaching Larry and Virginia's sense of peace.

Were they really where they were meant to be? Were the answers to their prayers seeking God's will really nearly 7 000 miles back there in Bonaire after all?

But instead of fearing, Larry and Virginia chose to wait patiently, still anchored in their sense of peace.

Finally, an airport employee approached them, bearing the news that the airport was closing, and they would have to leave the premises.

"There's a Holiday Inn not far away," he said, "and there's a shuttle that'll take you there."

Across the barren airport, there was no contact in sight. Only the stretch of well-trodden airport floors.

Stepping into the unknown, Larry and Virginia left the airport and stayed the night at the inn.

When daylight trickled through the hotel windows, they searched for a pay phone and found one, but Larry had no change, not even lodged in his deepest pockets, to pay for a call. Once again, the prospect of being stranded without any means of communication could have cast a cloud of discouragement over their minds. As they approached the telephone, however, they discovered to their astonishment the exact amount of change needed to make the call in the coin-return slot.

Larry McGuire and Ewart Hodgins standing in the antenna field at the Eswatini transmitter site.

The coin's glint reflected the hope in their hearts, serving as a tangible reminder that God was watching over them.

They made the call to the TWR Africa office and were greeted by the familiar voice of Dottie Simmonds, a missionary serving as administrator and secretary at the time. They informed her that they were at the Holiday Inn.

Her voice rippled with surprise. "What are you doing here? We sent a telegram to Monte Carlo to hold you there."

Just as they hadn't expected the South African winter, they hadn't expected that answer.

The telegram never arrived.

And lost, it never would.

This illustration depicts a simple method to test ground conductivity. Two metal rods are stuck in the ground at a certain distance apart from each other, calculated by the engineer. A power source, e.g. a battery or generator, etc., is connected to one rod and a current reader is connected to the other.

PUT TO WORK IMMEDIATELY

RIGHT AWAY, TWR began searching for the right piece of land in the southern African country for the building of the transmitter site, and the McGuires chose to stay, knowing that the new facility would come about in God's timing. On some days, Larry explored areas in the countries of Lesotho and Swaziland (whose name was later changed to Eswatini) to check ground-conductivity* levels. To Larry's

---

*Ground conductivity is how well the ground carries an electrical current. This is important for multiple purposes including how well the signal will "bounce" off of the ground.

amusement, some people suspected he and his co-workers were CIA agents driving stakes into the ground.

Other times, Larry gathered essential construction devices and created block-making equipment, knowing it was only a matter of time until the Lord provided the land for the transmitter site.

Sweet moments happened. The McGuires had their first child, Alan. And finally, after two years of long car rides from potential location to location that would trace a complicated webwork if mapped, the McGuires received news that evoked outpourings of praise from their hearts: The license to build a shortwave broadcasting site in Swaziland was approved.

A hoard of potential sites had already occupied their minds and deliberations. Then, soon after the license was approved, Larry and the team found Mpangela ranch for sale in Swaziland, located on a stretch of African bush that needed to be cleared.

HIS GUIDING HAND THROUGHOUT

PRESENTLY, THEY PURCHASED the land, not stopping to do ground-conductivity tests. Based on their deductions and previous visits, they believed it would be an ideal space to transmit radio signals, even into the remote corners of Africa where the gospel hadn't penetrated.

Years later, curiosity led the TWR missionaries in Swaziland to test those ground-conductivity levels. To their amazement, they found that the site had one of the highest ground-conductivity rates in the country.

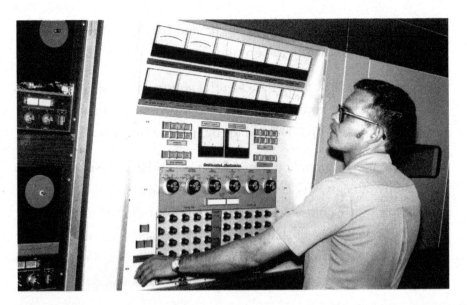

Larry McGuire monitoring broadcasts on a control panel of the playout system in the early 80s.

For Larry and Virginia, being a part of that nearly perfect outcome after all the uncertainties they and the TWR Africa team had faced was a testament to the importance of waiting on the Lord.

A telegram may have been lost along the way. But the purpose behind it wasn't misplaced. Rather, an all-knowing God held a purpose and plan through it all, guided by his loving care and wisdom.

He who plants and he who waters are one, and each will receive his wages according to his labor. For we are God's fellow workers. You are God's field, God's building.

1 Corinthians 3:8-9

2

Piecing the Transmitter Site Together

INSIDE THE MERRILY patterned paper, presents are also wrapped in anticipation. Exhilaration fused with wonder envelops children as they eagerly tear off the wrapping to unveil the treasures inside. Imagine, though, if the intensely anticipated item in the box were to turn out to be in pieces, a complicated jumble that would require lots of patience, time and effort to assemble before it could be enjoyed.

That's a lot like what TWR missionaries Larry and Virginia McGuire, along with other TWR staff members, experienced as they committed to building a radio site on the Mpangela Ranch in Eswatini (then known as Swaziland). Their experience was on a much greater scale, of course, and it encompassed challenging work and a gift immeasurably more fulfilling than a birthday novelty. And the gift giver was the Lord, the true provider of all good things.

Antenna towers are assembled in several sections to reach their full length of at least 30 meters. Pictured here is the Eswatini construction team raising the first section of a tower.

THE WORK BEGINS

A WILDERNESS OF dense shrubbery sprawled across hundreds of acres, covering virtually the entirety of Mpangela Ranch. The low tangle of African trees and bushes formed an intricate web of branches and was home to impalas, warthogs, kudu and zebras as well as several species of snakes, some venomous. Tan grass illuminated this wilderness when sunsets shifted the light browns to gold. Like opening a gift from God, Larry witnessed the divine provision of Mpangela Ranch, the chosen site for planting the transmitters, antennas, towers and everything else needed for broadcasting the gospel across large portions of sub-Saharan Africa.

In a Johannesburg storeroom roughly 250 miles from the ranch, five transmitters were tucked away. Four of them, each 25 000 watts and never used, had been manufactured in the 1940s and stored in a New York warehouse before being donated to TWR in 1970. The fifth transmitter, which was medium wave (AM) and 50 000 watts, was purchased from a company that had repossessed it from a bankrupt pirate-radio ship that once operated off the coasts of England and the Netherlands. God had provided this multipart gift, but there were more steps to take before all the pieces could be assembled so the gospel could be broadcast across Africa.

"Our first project was to build several miles of road to gain access or easier access to the property and clear several 100 acres of bush to make room for the buildings and antennas," says Larry.

A natural wall of plant life was a physical barrier to completing the transmitter site. But Larry knew that since the Lord had provided the land, he would enable the TWR staff to lay out a road to the ranch and clear the bushland where the broadcast towers would soon reach into the sky.

COMMISSIONED TO SERVE IN ESWATINI

In September 1973, Larry, Virginia and eldest son Allan relocated to the area in Eswatini as the summer season approached. Almost immediately, Larry and the TWR staff, comprising more than 30 families, set out to carve a road to the ranch. Simultaneously, others worked to establish a water system. Renting a massive bulldozer and hiring a driver, they began clearing the shrubby wilderness that they prayed

The team of engineers and technicians are assembling the transmitter control panels and working to get the shortwave transmitters ready for broadcasting.

would eventually house the transmitter site. Staff buildings were constructed within the vicinity, while apartments were rented in Manzini, which is the country's second-largest city and sometimes requires an hour's drive from the site.

The days seemed to stretch endlessly, as if time had expanded, adding extra hours of sunlight to the workdays. The weariness settled upon their bodies, burdening them like a heavy weight, and the task became monotonous at times – clearing shrubs meter by meter while starting to build the facilities on the site.

Larry toiled alongside other TWR missionary staff, enduring physical fatigue but noting the commitment burning inside each of them. It knit them together as a team, as Paul says in 1 Corinthians 12:12,

"Just as the body is one and has many members, and all the members of the body, though many, are one body, so it is with Christ." All were important in completing the Lord's work.

GOD'S FAITHFULNESS DESPITE OBSTACLES

AT TIMES, THE challenges loomed even taller than the towers they envisioned rising above the cleared fields of Mpangela Ranch. As they struggled to surmount the many barriers, the thought of those transmitters in Johannesburg awaiting instalment propelled them forward. Their goal burned like glowing embers in their hearts, radiating unity through their common focus.

Once enough land was cleared, Larry and his fellow missionaries began constructing the skeleton of a steel building. As the building neared completion, the team transferred the Johannesburg transmitters into the existing temporary structure, not only to save costs but also because they trusted that the day was drawing near when the transmitters could be installed. But then something unexpected happened that threatened to send the completion date further down the road.

For personal reasons, their original building contractor had to leave the project. Larry was an engineer, university trained to operate a radio station, but his skills didn't lie in that field alone. He had once worked in construction with his father, so hands-on building wasn't foreign to him.

Praise surged through the McGuires' hearts as they now better understood why that telegram telling them to stay in Monte Carlo had gone missing, as mentioned in the previous article: Part of the reason

God had brought him to Africa was to take over the construction process until another builder was found.

As some staff members used moulds to make cement building blocks, others continued to clear the field where the antennas would take the place of trees – like a technology orchard! They went on to erect the antennas, and transmission lines began to weave a pattern outside the building, gradually transforming the vision into a physical structure.

THE GOSPEL ON AIR

THE ROAD REQUIRED a couple of months to take shape, a primitive road that they understood would someday have to be improved. In November 1974, the team celebrated and praised God as the first transmitter officially went on air from the completed steel building. Another barrier had been overcome, allowing the gospel to pour out into hard-to-reach corners of Africa.

The process wasn't finished, however, for the transmitter building hadn't been completed and the other transmitters needed to be installed. Eventually, like scattered puzzle pieces falling into place, the pieces of the transmitter site converged, guided by the masterful hand of God. By early 1975, the transmitter building began to form, and they could transition the transmitters from the shed to a permanent building. New staff joined the endeavour, establishing a transmitter site where programmes could proclaim God's Word in multiple languages.

Through every obstacle standing between the clearing of the land and the building of the facilities, Larry witnessed the provision of God,

An aerial view of the TWR transmitter site, with the medium wave towers to the left and the shortwave antennas to the right. The photo was taken in the 80s.

faithful in even the most challenging and time-consuming moments. Like the unassembled birthday present, however, the Eswatini station emerged as a wonderful gift despite the challenge of having to build from the ground up. Even the building process alongside their TWR brothers and sisters was a cherished gift, for the McGuires saw the Lord use each staff member to complete the work.

"Six months from the initial on-air time, all four transmitters were being used for prime-time broadcasting all at once in over 20 languages," says Larry.

The believers had walked the journey together, and that journey continues in Eswatini as a testament to the power of God in believers, and as a reminded of the beauty of God's family, all focused on the same goal – to spread the gospel to the lost.

Trust in the Lord with all your heart, and do not lean on your own understanding. In all your ways acknowledge him, and he will make straight your paths.

Proverbs 3:5-6

3

Providential Patience and Problem-Solving

A S SOON AS he crossed the border between South Africa and Eswatini, Steve Stavropoulos found his small vehicle traversing an unpaved road, riddled with bumps. Though he was somewhat familiar with Eswatini, having participated in a high school mission trip there and driven through the landlocked kingdom then known as Swaziland to reach a holiday destination, nervousness crawled down his spine, an unease that seemed almost alive and driving with him in his vehicle.

The journey from Durban to the heart of Eswatini was over 500 kilometers (about 310 miles), but it wasn't the dirt road or the distance that particularly triggered the unease. Instead, the nervousness flared when his eyes rose to the sky, where a storm loomed, a dark billowing cloud that promised to release its contents at any moment. The vehicle crossed bridgeless streams as more clouds clogged the sky like coal-stained cotton. If the skies melted into a downpour, Steve knew, water would surge over cement drifts and render the route impassable.

Praying, he kept his vehicle in the center ridge of the road as he counted down the kilometers leading to the Manzini guesthouse where he'd be living during his week as a volunteer. As an engineering student, Steve needed practical experience as part of a university course, and it overjoyed him that he could use his skills in a gospel ministry.

What felt like endless kilometers later, his car arrived. The storm clouds hovered, the dark sky not yet releasing its fury.

VOLUNTEERING AT THE TWR TRANSMITTER SITE

RELIEF SATURATED HIM when he outran the rain and was greeted by Field Director Dick Olson, who welcomed him to a week of volunteering at the Trans World Radio transmitter site. Broadcasting had been underway only two months, and Steve's first glimpse of the site took in a small, unfinished building sitting within a clearing also occupied by an iron shed. Two shortwave transmitters labored inside the building, and a third transmitter was stationed on wooden pallets in the shed.

His week of volunteering was fulfilling. He not only learned new engineering skills but also experienced warm fellowship with the missionaries. He enjoyed the tasks even though they involved bouts of sprinting. When the broadcasts finished, he'd dash out of the building and into the shed. There, he'd manually switch off the third transmitter before returning to the main building.

In 2008 Steve Stavropolous went to the USA to evaluate whether a medium wave transmitter could have its frequency changed to 1170 kHz to replace the medium wave transmitter that had been in service in Eswatini since 1981.

Before his week at the transmitter site, he sensed that the Lord might be calling him to missions, but the pathway to missions was hazy. A couple of months after Steve finished his degree, the Lord cleared the haze and the pathway to missionary service. After learning about a shortage of engineers at the fledgling transmitter site where he had volunteered, Steve realized that the Lord was calling him back to Eswatini. Back at the TWR site in May 1977, just over two years after he had first worked there, he saw changes. The transmitter was no longer in the shed, and the building's size had expanded. Not only that, but the site now received electricity via power lines rather than having to rely on generators.

FINDING AN EFFICIENT TECHNOLOGY

BUT ONE ASPECT had stayed the same. And it remained that way for the next 10 years he served at the Eswatini station. It was the process of turning on and off the transmitters.

"It was very hands-on, and for the evening shift, it was quite complicated. We really needed three people – two operators and an engineer on duty," says Steve.

With the shortwave transmitters, the frequency had to be adjusted so the signal would reach particular countries according to the time of day. This often coincided with a change in programme language. One person would climb inside the transmitter – a blue metal box containing assorted electronic components. He'd follow a chart to unscrew coils, taking out and plugging in capacitors to change the frequency. Another person stood outside, manipulating external levers while winding and turning knobs to configure the system, and a third member of the technical staff stood by to address any problems that arose. In addition, the staff's duties included swapping the tapes on tape machines as the reels ended, switching to the audio on the next machine.

In a day's work, three shifts of people came to operate the transmitters. A morning shift left Manzini, the nearby town where staff quarters were located, about 3:45 am to start the transmitters at 4:30 am. The day shift arrived around 7:00 am and the evening shift around lunchtime. They operated until midnight and drove home in the darkness.

These photos depict the typical roles that needed to be filled during a broadcasting shift opperating the short wave (SW) transmitters.

Above Left: Dennis Fogo making an adjustment in the tuning network inside of a 25 kW SW transmitter.

Above Right: Steve Platt tuning a 25 kW SW transmitter from the front panel.

Right: Eric Ndlovu in the playout center, during an evening shift, with the 25 kW SW transmitters in background.

Steve felt there had to be a more efficient method to change frequencies. The existing process wasn't the best use of an engineer's skills, because it pulled him away from the daytime shift, when the transmitters were off the air and he could be conducting technical testing, maintenance and experimentation. The solution, however, was a mystery to him.

As the years rolled by, so did the monotonous, time-consuming nature of operating the transmitters. A desire for a solution gnawed at him. Sometimes, a sense of discouragement threatened to consume him, but he turned to the Lord and was granted persistence, cultivating his patience throughout the years.

One day, a co-worker approached Steve, slapping down a magazine on his desk. From a glance, Steve could see that it was an engineering or broadcast magazine. Among the articles on the pages, he spotted a hand-drawn circle over a certain term: programmable logic controller.

"This is it," his co-worker said. "This is what we need."

After some studying, Steve discovered that a PLC is a device that controls relays and switches in fruit packing and factory production. Factory operators write instructional programmes that switch controls on and off. Steve's determination to get hold of the technology stirred to life.

ACHIEVING A COMMON GOAL

A SHARED MOTIVATION emerged among the staff: "Let's go for it!" Steve began to investigate, finding not only a supplier who

40

provided training but a sugar mill that used the supplier's PLC. It was in a town about two and a half hours north of the transmitter site, so Steve contacted the chief technical officer at the mill to request a visit. Amid sugar cane being dumped, cut and squashed as rollers and boilers warbled and harmonized like a choir in the background, Steve and the team learned the basics of the PLC.

Steve and the team gradually integrated the system into the site, feeding it more and more programmes. Gradually, the three-operator system shrank to one operator per shift, and efficiency and productivity grew. Despite initial challenges faced during the adjustment period, the team found solace in the Lord's provision of strength and patience, enabling them to overcome any obstacles encountered along the way.

Two years after officially joining TWR, Steve married Lorraine, and the Lord blessed the couple with three cherished children – Esther, Duane and John – all born at the mission hospital in Eswatini. Eventually, he became chief engineer, a role he held for 18 years before the couple moved to West Africa, where he served as engineer. In 2018 Steve became station director back in Eswatini, with plans to turn over those duties to a successor in 2020 while remaining involved as an adviser and assisting with special projects.

From installing new antennas and transmitters to repairing torn feed lines to tracking down an efficient PLC solution, Steve witnessed the unwavering faithfulness of the Lord. Steve often found himself asking God for wisdom, and God always provided – even on the dark roads endangered by storms or the paved roads winding through sunlit valleys.

The Lord is my light and my salvation;
whom shall I fear?
The Lord is the stronghold of my life;
of whom shall I be afraid?

Psalm 27:1

4

Their Call Came in the Night

I T WAS ABOUT 9 p.m. The phone rang at the home of Evert and Edie Kleynhans in South Africa.

Was it true that Evert was a Christian builder? the caller asked. It was 1973 or possibly early 1974. The caller was from Swaziland (now Eswatini). A missionary organization called Trans World Radio was in the midst of a building project, and its staff could use some help.

Might the Kleynhanses be available for a temporary assignment? Yes, they would.

"We came on as temporary," Edith, (generally known as "Edie") Kleynhans said in a 2014 video interview with TWR's Andrew Haas. "Temporary turned into quite long. Because there was always something more to do."

MISSIONS DRIVEN

ALTHOUGH THE KLEYNHANSES hadn't sought the assignment, serving in missions was certainly embedded in their DNA.

Edie Kleinschmidt was born in 1928 in the Democratic Republic of Congo, then a Belgian colony, to Africa Inland Mission medical missionary parents, according to her obituary. Her schooling began at Rethy Academy in Congo. (Former students say expatriates evacuated the area in the late 1990s, and the facility was never reopened as a school for missionary kids.)

At Rethy Academy, Edie met a boy named Evert Kleynhans. Evert, whose parents were South African, also was the child of missionaries in Congo.

Edie would return to Congo and marry Evert in 1957. But before that, she went to the United States to finish high school in Florida and then continued her education at Moody Bible Institute in Chicago, followed by Wheaton College in Illinois and then at New York University, where she earned her nursing degree.

STARTING THEIR JOURNEY TOGETHER

AFTER MARRYING, THE couple settled on a farm in Congo and started a family. Their first three children, Coralee, Andries and Rosemarie, were born on the farm, but the Congo crisis forced them to leave in 1963. They made the overland move to Durban, South Africa, where Evert set up a construction business specializing in church buildings. Their fourth child, George, was born there.

Evert Kleyhans discussing building plans for the transmitter site in 1974.
Left to right: Walter Dien, Evert Kleyhans, Dave Nordquist, Jonathan Gain

Evert Kleynhans sitting in a borehole water pump house which is under construction in 1977. He is working with two local members of the building team.

Although that nighttime call in the early '70s was a surprise, Trans World Radio was known to the couple. Edie said she had learned of it through founder Paul Freed and his wife, Betty Jane.

They said yes and arrived on an 18-month assignment mostly to build the transmittering station. However, they went on to serve with TWR for 17 years and participated in building projects in several southern Africa countries before retiring in 1991.

Edith Kleynhans, photo taken in 2014 during her interview with Andrew Haas.

FOND MEMORIES

YEARS LATER, EDIE Kleynhans still had warm memories of that initial assignment.

"The Lord provided staff that were from all sorts of countries," she told Haas during the interview at Glenhaven Retirement Centre in Pretoria, South Africa. "And we became such close family friends, the TWR family. It was too marvelous to see the Lord's hand at work in so many, many ways. You never knew what he was going to do next, but the way he answered prayer in that building – sometimes it was people needed, sometimes it was supplies needed."

That first project culminated on Nov. 1, 1974.

"The opening day, that was really exciting," she said. "Everybody was really excited. Because now this is the real thing, and it's going to go on the air. So that was a very special, special day. Everybody was just thanking the Lord for what had been done."

Ruth (Schuit) Carter remembers Edie and Evert revisiting Rethy Academy years later and speaking in a student chapel when she was a student there.

"I remember Evert introducing Edith as 'the one most precious to me,'" Carter wrote. "As an elementary-age girl, I thought that was so romantic and sweet to hear!"

After retiring, the Kleynhanses settled at Glenhaven Retirement Centre, where Evert passed away in 2005. Edie died at the age of 93 on May 1, 2022. Her family said she spent her final days singing the hymn "Count Your Blessings" and reciting John 3:16-17:

For God so loved the world, that he gave his only Son, that whoever believes in him should not perish but have eternal life. For God did not send his Son into the world to condemn the world, but in order that the world might be saved through him.

How then will they call on him in whom they have not believed? And how are they to believe in him of whom they have never heard? And how are they to hear without someone preaching?

Romans 10:14

5

The 'Africa Challenge' of Stephen Boakye-Yiadom

GOD CALLED STEPHEN Boakye-Yiadom to Germany to send him back to Africa. He became God's instrument in bringing the gospel to Africa through media.

Born in Ghana, where he completed his schooling, Boakye-Yiadom was working at a bank when he decided to continue his studies abroad.

That took him to Germany, where he met Herta Wojahn, whom he came to refer to as his foster mother. At her home, Boakye-Yiadom heard a broadcast from Evangeliums Rundfunk (ERF) on the subject "What can we do for Africa?"

He recalled thinking that if Germans wanted to do something for Africa, it would not do for an African to sit around idly.

Grace Boakye-Yiadom with Herta Wojahn, Stephen's adopted German mother and Rev. Stephen Boakye-Yiadom. This photo was taken in Nairobi, Kenya, in 1978.

MOVING INTO MINISTRY

THAT LED TO a meeting in 1972 or '73 with the Rev. Horst Marquardt, a founding member and director of ERF, which is TWR's national partner in Germany. Wojahn and Heinz Storberg, an evangelist on the ERF committee, also were there.

"I told Stephen, should we ever work there [in Africa] and should he want to help us there, he would need an education in theology and journalism," Marquardt recalled.

Boakye-Yiadom answered the call, enrolling in Chrischona Theological Seminary in Switzerland, being ordained in the Methodist

Church and, in September 1975, joining ERF as an intern under Marquardt. A year later, he was back in Africa, where he was sent to lead a new TWR office in Nairobi, Kenya. Together with TWR, he launched the *Africa Challenge* programme.

After being appointed regional director for TWR Africa in 1992, Boakye-Yiadom, his wife, Grace, and their four children moved to Johannesburg. Later, his title was changed to international director for TWR Africa, a post he held until his sudden death due to heart failure on June 2, 2007. He was TWR's first native international director for Africa.

Steven Boakye-Yiadom and Tom Tatlow, long-time TWR missionary in Africa, at a transmitter site located south of Johannesburg, South Africa, that has since been decommissioned.

LEAVING A LEGACY OF LOVE

BOAKYE-YIADOM WAS KNOWN for having the true heart of a father and for his warm hugs, passion for sharing the gospel and often-repeated maxim, "Africa needs Jesus!"

James Burnett, who has served with TWR in Africa since 1982, described him like this: "He was such a wonderful people person who loved people. You could never hold anything against him."

Becky Uhden, a leader on the financial side for TWR Africa for 23 years, said Boakye-Yiadom "was a man of God who was a good leader. He led the ministry in Africa with joy and hard work."

His children summed up the work of Stephen in a statement after his death:

"Our father's life was filled with the desire to bring the Word of God to the people of Africa."

O Lord God, you have only begun to show
your servant your greatness and your mighty hand.
For what god is there in heaven or on earth who
can do such works and mighty acts as yours?

Deuteronomy 3:24

6

A 'Short-term' Missionary Goes Long

BECKY UHDEN WAS asked to serve with TWR in Africa for two years.

She stayed for 23.

"Becky may hold the record for the longest short term of missionary service in TWR," wrote Tom Streeter, one of TWR's longest-serving missionaries.

Streeter wasn't referring to Uhden's service in Africa so much as to her "short term" that started even before that.

Uhden, who "retired" in 2016 as Africa Regional Office finance director, had the financial expertise that made her much needed in the mission field combined with a heart of obedience to God that prompted her to accept the call.

HEEDING THE CALL

ALL OF THIS started in 1976, when Uhden was working in the office of her church in Spokane, Washington, in the U.S. She received a letter from her sister, Elly Streeter, Tom's wife. The assistant in the Finance Department for TWR in Monte Carlo, where the Streeters were serving, was going on furlough the next year. Could Becky come and fill in for a short term?

Accountant Becky Uhden verifying billing data in Monte Carlo in 1981.

In a sense, Uhden already had given her answer as a result of a missions conference she had attended as a teenager at her church. "I told the Lord that I was willing to do and go anywhere he wanted me to serve," she recalled.

Uhden applied to TWR for short-term ministry and was 27 when she arrived in Monte Carlo for a six-month term. While she was there, the Lord led her to apply for full-time service. She returned home to raise support then settled in at Monte Carlo, first as an assistant and later as field treasurer.

While still in Monte Carlo, Uhden was asked to spend three months in Swaziland – now Eswatini – working with the three members of their Finance Team. Seeds may have been planted then, but Uhden returned to Monte Carlo on schedule. In 1987, she was transferred to the European Regional Office in The Netherlands to serve as regional treasurer for TWR Europe.

NEEDED IN AFRICA

WHILE SHE WAS there, the international director for Europe and Africa came to their office after visiting the Africa Regional Office. "He made the comment, 'They need a Becky in Africa,'" Uhden recalled. "We laughed at that statement and that was that."

Only it wasn't, because the international director shared a devotional with the staff that the Lord used to work in Uhden's heart. It led her to think there might be a change, she said. A few months later, in 1993, Uhden was asked if she would be willing to go to Africa for up to two years to help set up the Finance Department for the Africa Regional Office. That was the two-year commitment that turned into 23.

During her time with TWR, Uhden saw her work go from manual accounting to using an account software programme. She saw TWR programmes move from reel-to-reel tapes to cassettes to CDs to computers and eventually the internet. Communication changed from letters to phone, to telex to telegrams to faxes and then online.

One of the biggest challenges during her time in Africa was when TWR worked to start up the West Africa transmitter site. "I looked back at some of my prayer letters, and it seemed like forever for the license, the station, the equipment shipments, clearing customs and such to go through," she wrote.

Regional Accountant Becky Uhden working in the TWR Africa's first office in Kempton Park, South Africa, in 1995.

She enjoyed visiting national offices and seeing how quickly the teams would grasp training in new financial methods. She took delight in attending the 25th anniversary celebration in Swaziland.

"I developed friendships with some great people through the years – in TWR as well as local people in the places where I lived," Uhden wrote. "The downside of the friendships were the sad goodbyes when people left, or I moved to the other locations."

The feeling was mutual.

"The mother of TWR Africa," Anthony Barkhuizen said of Uhden.

"Becky was our 'go to' person," said Barkhuizen, who has served with TWR Africa along with his wife, Karen, since 2001. "If we needed to know something – ask Becky. She knew things! She also cared for us. In the absence of a resident regional leader, Becky made sure we had regular social times, and she provided the best hot chocolate mix in winter. Her soup and bread-roll days and the social times were legendary.

"Becky switched the lights on in the morning and switched them off at night. Becky is missed."

When Uhden, now 73, left Africa in 2016 and returned to the United States it was to retire, but not to quit working. She again works in her church's office, volunteering two days a week. Her attention to detail pays off in a service she provides for the multilingual website TWR360.

"She routinely audits the site, language by language, ministry by ministry, sending me spreadsheets of her findings," wrote longtime TWR missionary Jim Hill, now a member of the TWR360 administrative team. "At times, she sends emails alerting me to more pressing problems. She is a much-appreciated assistant in my work with a heart to continue to reach people in their heart languages."

Uhden's lifetime of faithful service, in Africa and elsewhere, fits well with the Scripture she cites as her life verse, Philippians 2:13:

For it is God who works in you,
both to will and to work for his good pleasure.

I press on toward the goal for the prize of the
upward call of God in Christ Jesus.

Philippians 3:14

7

Passion for Radio, Passion for Jesus

T HE 12-YEAR-OLD BOY listened to the messages coming into his shortwave radio, fascinated.

It was 1956, and in a dispute with other nations, Egyptian President Gamal Abdel Nasser had blocked the Suez Canal by ordering his troops to sink 40 ships. This meant all shipping was diverted around the Cape of Good Hope.

Young Andrew MacDonald, from his boyhood home in Cape Town, South Africa, witnessed the traffic via ship-to-shore radio, he wrote in an unpublished memoir. A year later, he would join radio enthusiasts from around the world tracking shortwave signals from the Soviet Union's Sputnik satellite.

But as an adult, the Rev. Andrew MacDonald would be involved in radio not from ships or from satellites but from the most powerful source of all: the Word of God.

AN EARLY INTEREST IN RADIO

BORN 21 DECEMBER 1943 and born again at a Youth for Christ event in 1961, MacDonald came by his interest in radio naturally. He joined the family radio engineering business in 1963 while studying for his radio engineering qualification at night.

He also learned to play the organ, and he became organist and choirmaster at Metropolitan Methodist Church in Cape Town. He married Barbara there in 1968. They would have three children: David, Steaphan and John.

Later, he filled the same positions at Cape Town Baptist Church. That's where he learned that Trans World Radio was looking for a place to establish a radio station in what was then Swaziland and is now called Eswatini.

"The chief engineer Bob Shultz and his wife, Ethelyn, were on holiday in Cape Town and attended Sunday service at Cape Town Baptist Church, where I was organist and choirmaster," MacDonald wrote. "Ethelyn, being a musician, came and spoke to me at the organ and mentioned that her husband was busy investigating the best site for the proposed shortwave station."

THE CALL TO TWR

MACDONALD WASN'T PART of TWR when the first official broadcast was heard from Manzini, Swaziland, on 4 November 1974, although he had caught some test broadcasts the previous month.

From left to right: Amos Kitner, Andrew MacDonald, Dick Olson, Paul Freed, Mr. Mamba, and Swazi staff members in traditional dress at the 10th anniversary celebration of TWR Africa in 1984.

Andrew and Barbara joined TWR in 1977, after he spent a year in Bible college. For two years they served out of Cape Town, where they set up studios with an office and produced 10 programmes a week. Then they were transferred to Manzini on a one-year assignment. That grew to 14 years, as Andrew served first under the programme director, then as programme director and finally as director of ministry development. Barbara assisted in the Finance Department.

While serving in Manzini, Andrew continued his studies and was ordained at Cape Town Baptist Church in 1990.

Stephen Boakye-Yiadom, Andrew MacDonald, and Tom Lowell, former TWR president, standing in front of transmitters in Meyerton, South Africa.

SETTING UP IN SOUTH AFRICA

THEIR MANZINI ASSIGNMENT lasted until 1992, when the MacDonalds were asked to open the new Africa Regional Office – and to figure out where that office would be. After visits to Zimbabwe, Malawi, Mozambique and Kenya, they decided South Africa would be best. The site they bought was in Kempton Park, the city where the Africa Regional Office remains today.

In Kempton Park, Barbara helped set up the regional office and the Africa Institute in Christian Communication and directed the TWR Audience Relations department. Andrew served as director of ministry for Africa until July 1995 and then served as a consultant to TWR.

Even while being treated for cancer in 2005, Andrew remained involved with and enthused about the work of TWR Africa.

"Since our first days with TWR, right up to the present, we rejoice when a listener finds Jesus Christ as Saviour through our radio programmes," he wrote at the time. "Just last week we heard of 18 people who came to Christ in Bulawayo, Zimbabwe, as a result of listening to *Thru the Bible* in Zulu. This is what motivates us in our service with TWR."

Andrew MacDonald passed into glory on 12 July 2007.

Blessed is the man who trusts in the Lord,

whose trust is the Lord.

He is like a tree planted by water,

that sends out its roots by the stream,

and does not fear when heat comes,

for its leaves remain green,

and is not anxious in the year of drought,

for it does not cease to bear fruit.

Jeremiah 17:7-8

8

Bridging the Changes in Audio Technology

A SWING BRIDGE, built of used mining steel cables and a wooden pathway that was suspended by diamond mesh fencing, extends over a muddy river that is knotted with interlocking trees, bushes and plants. The river curves into the distance, its destination hidden by the dense shrubbery.

Along the riverbank, miracles happened. During the initial construction of the transmitting station in Eswatini (then called Swaziland), the Lord provided one of those amazing thunderstorms that caused the river to flood and deposit sand onto the shores. The sand was just what the TWR staff had been praying for to make the concrete for construction!

In the days after, the river and its banks were at the heart of another milestone in TWR history.

A wheelbarrow rocked across the bridge in the mid-1970s. Blue steel boxes were tucked in the wheelbarrow, containing newly recorded audio tapes. Although the swing bridge wasn't nearly as rigid as a solid bridge, the staff's steps as they pushed the barrow across it were careful and focused. The reel-to-reel audiotapes were being transported to the recently built station, where the recorded programmes would be broadcast across the region over shortwave transmitters.

The swing bridge over the Mbuluzane River. While this photo was taken in 1973, when the site was under construction, this bridge is still used.

TRANSPORTING AND BROADCASTING THE GOSPEL

JAMES BURNETT, A shift engineer who joined TWR in 1982, joined existing staff members in lugging the boxes across the bridges whenever the low-level car bridge was flooded by summer thunderstorms. As bulky as the boxes were, and as narrow as the bridge was, this was still the only means for conveying the audio tapes to the transmitter site when the river was high. And behind those audio tapes, beyond even the process of recording them, was the process of crossing the border, a custom process that often-encompassed barriers, stress,

James Burnett working the night shift at the Eswatini transmitting station in October of 1986. He is putting one-hour tapes on to the tape machines. These tapes hold the programmes that were aired that evening.

and unease, for at times, the border customs seemed to make it their goal to create difficulty for the TWR equipment.

"In those days, the tape machines and the computers, we had to hand-carry in. It was very stressful going through customs," James says.

Once the tapes were ready to be used in the station, the audio operator positioned the tapes on the tape machines, manually changing them every hour to switch to different programmes. James witnessed the switch from analogue to digital, and the process of transporting the tape machines over the swing bridge passed into history, allowing the engineers more time and space to fulfil other tasks at the transmitter site.

Lyn Burnett recording announcements from a script in the early '90s.

RECORDING THE GOSPEL

LYN BURNETT STARTED broadcasting announcements in 1987, about five years after she and her husband, James, joined TWR. She saw not only the reel-to-reel machines disappear but also significant changes in the recording process. Rather than recording the announcements in TWR's high-tech-filled studios, they were recorded in a tiny soundproof room in the TWR offices onto reel-to-reel machines four times a year. The announcements were then put onto cart machines, from which they were inserted between the programmes. The programmes, together with the announcements, were put onto big reel-to-reel tapes that each held an hour's worth of programmes.

Many years later, Lyn was recording onto a computer in the Kempton Park* office rather than a tape recorder. She still mostly read from a script and voiced the same kind of announcements that she had before, but instead of prerecording them four times a year, she did them each week, resulting in their sounding more relevant and "live." She discovered that her speech captured on the computer sounded more natural and conversational. Recording on the old tapes seemed more confined somehow, and the simpler, streamlined audio editing on the computer allowed for more experimentation and flexibility.

"Instead of cutting and splicing if you made a mistake and then putting the tape back together, it was all done on the computer," Lyn says. "The editing was just cut and paste. It was much more fun, and it sounded more live, although we weren't live. ... You can make it sound quite real and natural, and so that aspect really developed over the years."

GOD'S HAND IN EVERY TECHNOLOGICAL TRANSITION

THE BURNETTS EXPERIENCED the era before recorded programmes were transported to the Eswatini station over the internet and even before that when they were carried on USB devices. But as

---

*TWR Africa's main office originally was in a house on Willow Street, Kempton Park, close to Johannesburg International Airport. It was only in 1996 when regionalization took place that the operations were slowly moved, step-by-step, to the current regional corporate offices, also situated in Kempton Park, South Africa.

technological bridges replaced the old methods, like the wooden swing bridge and wheelbarrow, TWR explored each advancement to see if it could be leveraged to make operations more efficient and effective. Throughout TWR's 50 years in sub-Saharan Africa, the Lord has guided the Burnetts and their co-workers through these transitions, granting them the wisdom and perseverance to improve and grow the ministry.

Scripture has been a rock and signpost in the Burnetts' lives. A favourite verse is Psalms 23:6, "Surely goodness and mercy shall follow me all the days of my life." The Burnetts cling to the guidance and promise of Proverbs 3:5-6, "Trust in the Lord with all your heart, and do not lean on your own understanding. In all your ways acknowledge him, and he will make straight your paths."

"That's kind of been our guideline and theme, and we've also learned that to trust God is an ongoing process – to learn to trust him," James says. "And he proved it true over the 40 years with TWR, that you can trust the Lord, and he looks after you and cares for you. So, we've learned and proved the dependability of God in our lives. As we look back at the 40 years, he's looked after us and cared for us, met all our needs, and has been a real, real Father to us. This was true even during the very difficult time when our 18-year-old son was killed in a road accident. As we look back, we can see the Lord had brought us through."

I have great sorrow and unceasing anguish in my heart. For I could wish that I myself were accursed and cut off from Christ for the sake of my brothers, my kinsmen according to the flesh. ... My heart's desire and prayer to God for them is that they may be saved.

Romans 9:2-3; 10:1

9

Makeshift Studio Brings God's
Word to West Africa

UNDER THE ROOF of his Côte d'Ivoire home, the Rev. Abdoulaye Sangho toiled on his knees in a room that had once been a child's bedroom. Using old egg cartons he had collected, he lined each section of the room's walls. Already, he'd spent countless hours labouring in the room, heated by the African sun, and those hours strung together to form long days. To the eye, the room was hardly grand, but he was transforming it into a room fit for a palace. From here, the words of Christ the King would soon be proclaimed to West Africa.

If a stranger had wandered into the room and caught Abdoulaye on his knees carefully attaching egg cartons to the wall, he may have believed that the minister had lost his senses, but that would be far from the truth. The idea was for the knobby cardboard-style cartons to act as a form of soundproofing and sound absorption to improve

Rev. Abdoulaye Sangho wearing traditional West African clothing.

the acoustics of the room. For he was converting the room into a recording studio.

A love for West Africans filled his heart, and the depth of his love emanated from his own experience. He shared a background with many of them, steeped in Islam and influenced by African traditional practices. How he yearned for West African Muslims to hear about Jesus Christ like he had as a teen! And that desire is why he was working on his knees to transform a child's bedroom into a homemade studio. In that room, the first TWR programme recorded in West Africa to reach out to the Muslim community for Christ would be made.

TOOTHACHE LEADS TO NEW LIFE

ABDOULAYE SPENT HIS childhood in Mali surrounded by the teachings of Islam, which had thrived there for centuries. Immersed in a country where little outside religious influence seeped in, his childhood lacked the joy of Christ.

At a young age, Abdoulaye experienced profound losses that smothered the early life he had known, like a hand snuffing out every source of light in a home. By the age of 10, he had lost both his parents and his grandparents, leaving him an orphan. During his teenage years, however, he encountered a missionary couple who treated him as if he were their own son, and it started with Abdoulaye suffering overwhelming pain.

Pain radiated across his mouth and at night robbed him of sleep, leaving him exhausted throughout the day. It continued after sunrise, becoming almost unbearable. He had two molars riddled with cavities, and he realised he needed to see a dentist as soon as possible to quell the pain.

Little did he know when he entered the dentist's office that another, more debilitating, type of pain would also be healed. It was a wound he had carried since birth: a life without Christ.

The dentist was a Baptist missionary from the United States who spoke the local language and had lived in town for over 10 years. He shared the gospel with Abdoulaye, who had never talked with a Christian before. The young man absorbed each word and afterward delightedly accepted a set of Christian booklets and Bible magazines from the kind-hearted man.

Later, he flipped through each page, soaking in the new truths and contemplating them throughout the day. Along with the Christian literature, the missionary and his wife poured their love and kindness into him as if they were his parents, sharing truths from Scriptures.

As Abdoulaye read, conviction flooded his chest, bringing him to the realisation that he needed to accept Jesus as his Lord and Saviour. This act set him apart from the people around him in predominantly Muslim Mali.

He couldn't bottle up the gospel inside him, and his new faith was noticed in the community. The community's perceptions of Abdoulaye changed as he changed. He began to be known for his faith, and his peers heard the gospel, many for the very first time. Because the teachings he now believed were different from the ones they held, Abdoulaye's teachers sought him out with lots of questions.

His heart especially ached for four close friends he attended school with. Praying for them, he dedicated himself to sharing the gospel with them, and through the miraculous hand of God, three were saved.

A passion was kindled inside those friends. They, too, eagerly shared the gospel with the community.

"Two became pastors and Bible teachers like I did, and the third friend became one of the pillars of the Evangelical Baptist Church of Diré, in northern Mali," Abdoulaye testifies.

God had additional answered prayers in store for Abdoulaye, opening doors for him to proclaim Christ not only to the people of Mali but also those in the much larger arena of West Africa.

MINISTERING TO WEST AFRICANS BY RADIO

FOUR YEARS PASSED, and Abdoulaye's love for the Lord still burned brightly, along with his desire to reach the lost around him. God led him out of his home country to attend a Bible college in Côte d'Ivoire. He moved to the new country, and after four years of training at the college, Abdoulaye graduated and joined a radio ministry called Eternal Love Winning Africa (best known as ELWA) that focused on sharing the Scriptures with West Africans. There, he became a radio pastor and programme producer. The responses of listeners to the ministry were miraculous, blessing the young broadcaster with a joy that couldn't be surpassed – he was fulfilling the calling to serve his beloved West Africans.

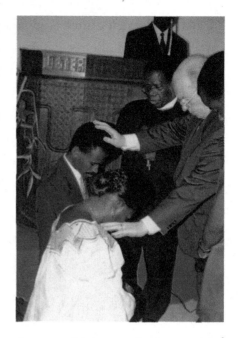

A prayer of dedication for Rev. Abdoulaye Sangho and his wife as they joined TWR in 1997, by the Rev. Dr. Andre Kouakou Kouadio, president of both the CMA and the Evangelical Federation of Côte d'Ivoire, and Rev. Horst Marquardt of ERF.

Not only was spiritual fruit produced, but the Lord used the time to train him in voice production and pastoring. In January 1996, he was invited to join the staff of TWR, a growing global Christian media ministry that had been in partnership with ELWA. West Africa had become a space without Christian broadcasting after ELWA's station in Liberia was destroyed in 1990 during a war that racked the country. TWR, already reaching out to much of the continent from its Eswatini (then known as Swaziland) transmitters, wanted to step up its presence and gospel outreach in this region. After six months of praying, receiving godly counsel, wisdom and encouragement from his wife, he decided it was God's desire for him to join TWR.

On Oct. 1, 1996, after Abdoulaye finished attaching the last egg carton to the wall, he recorded the TWR programme *Africa Challenge* in French, the first TWR programme recorded and aired in West Africa. Recording the programme, which focused on building up West Africans' spiritual lives in the Lord and tackled a variety of cultural topics, also heralded the founding of TWR's national partner in Côte d'Ivoire, now known as Radio Évangile. Broadcasting from a short-wave transmitter in Johannesburg, a space for French-speaking Africans to hear the good news of Jesus Christ was created.

TWR'S OUTREACH IN WEST AFRICA GROWS

ABDOULAYE CONTINUALLY EXPERIENCED God's grace as the region's ministry grew, and he was eventually called to become the TWR international director for West and Central Africa, called WeCAf for short.

He watched as the makeshift, egg-carton recording room gave way to a proper, purpose-built studio for the production of many programmes. Today, the programmes encompass more than 35 languages and dialects, and the West Africa Transmitting Station, launched in 2008, now broadcasts gospel programming over two powerful medium wave (AM) signals. The transmitter known as 'Oasis' focuses on the continent's most-populous country, Nigeria, and surrounding areas, while the other covers much of the rest of the region. The huge potential Muslim audience is served with programmes such as *Talmatha, The Way of Righteousness, Oasis of Hope* and *The Prophets*, the last programme written and produced by Abdoulaye.

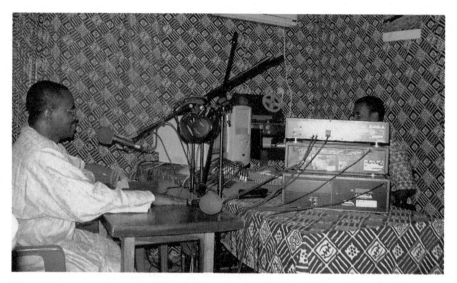

Rev. Abdoulaye Sangho and the *Thru The Bible* Pulaar producer working in the very first West Africa makeshift studio in Côte d'Ivoire in 1997.

Throughout the years, he has experienced God's powerful hand on his life and on the ministry of TWR, but most precious to him is the knowledge that God is using him and the ministry he leads to reach out to Muslims across West Africa.

"But above all, hearing the testimony of men and women rooted in traditional religions and Islam now worshipping the one true and living God through Jesus Christ is a special grace," he says.

The heart of man plans his way,
but the Lord establishes his steps.

Proverbs 16:9

10

A Blessing in a Bungalow: God's Direction for Eberhard

I N A BUNGALOW not far from Cape Town, South Africa, Eberhard Haberkorn's interest in computers grew from a tiny seed to a thriving sapling. It was an unlikely place to cultivate an interest in technology, for the bungalow housed several South African infantry conscripts having registered with a university or college in the late 1980s. Technology like computers wasn't common in such a setting. Nor was it usually allowed.

But God used this set of circumstances to steer Eberhard onto a path where he could serve the Lord with his heart for the lost.

Eberhard Haberkorn (left) and the Englishman (Llewelen Edgerton) he shared a bungalow with in the army working on an anti-aircraft radar and gun system that tracked enemy planes.

A PATH STEERED FOR EBERHARD

EBERHARD HAD ALREADY spent a few months in his compulsory two- year military service, and compared with other military barracks in which he had stayed, the bungalow was a luxury hotel. His harshest accommodation was a barrack built of corrugated iron in the middle of winter. An opening in the roof let in fresh air, and the men shared one room below, each bundled in his sleeping bag. The cold winter robbed the men of sleep, but Eberhard fought back. He'd get into the bag fully clothed along with extra blankets, but the cold still penetrated the barrack and seeped into his bones no matter how many layers he added.

Then, he got transferred to a bungalow at the Signals unit, in Cape Town, where only two men shared a room. Along with a kitchen and living space, the bungalow had better insulation to keep them warm on cold days.

While the conditions were better, the real highlight of these quarters was one of his English bunkmate's possessions. for it would turn out to be a key factor in God's direction for Eberhard's life. The bunkmate owned a 1987 Apple computer.

Eberhard got along well with the Englishman – unlike an earlier experience when one of the infantry conscripts wouldn't stop playing heavy metal music. Forming a friendship with Eberhard, the Englishman spent spare moments introducing the workings of his Apple computer. The boxy device had a keyboard and a linear space where data-storing floppy disks were inserted.

"He actually taught me a lot of stuff from there, and then my interest in computers grew," says Eberhard.

Noting Eberhard's fascination with the device, the bunkmate let him tinker with its workings, and his interest flared even more. It continued to flourish along with his growing usage of computers, eventually leading him to an office in Pretoria that put technology to work reaching Africa for Christ.

SERVING THE LORD BY PURSUING NEW INTERESTS

IN 1990, EBERHARD joined TWR as a studio technician. He edited and maintained the programming for German-speaking listeners in Africa, but as his interest shifted to new areas, he found himself on the artistic side of technology. Becoming

Eberhard Haberkorn working in TWR South Africa's studios in the early '90s.

Step 1: The first step of putting the newsletter together in the '90s was to design the layout of the newsletters on the computer using QuarkXPress.

Step 2: The next step was to print out the design and look for suitable photos and illustrations. The images were cut to size and shape and arranged and glued on to the newsletter printout. These pages were then taken to a printing company.

a graphic designer, he formed and assembled images for the TWR Africa newsletter, and this provided a brimming sense of enjoyment. In his work, he shaped ideas into designs. Then, he formatted those designs into printed newsletters that showcased the Lord working across Africa through testimonies, updates and prayers. But designing wasn't always easy, for advanced design software wasn't available at the time, making it hard to turn the designs he imagined into reality.

In charge of designing and printing newsletters, Eberhard gathered old films and massive printing sheets, along with the meticulously cut-out photos. He pasted them on sheets, carefully arranging them in designs that would format appropriately in print. The process was painstaking at times, but Eberhard didn't consider quitting. The challenge invigorated him, especially knowing that the newsletter he was producing would be distributed far and wide to bless listeners and supporters across Africa. Starting in 1996, Eberhard worked mostly on snail-mail newsletters until the early 2000s, when email started rolling out throughout the continent. Eberhard witnessed the shift from physical newsletters arriving in mailboxes to ones appearing in email inboxes instead. While the postal system declined in many places, the efficiency and popularity of email rose.

Not only did the use of email climb, but Eberhard also saw design software become increasingly sophisticated, from software like Ventura Publisher to AMI Pro, and those later replaced by QuarkXPress. With each new software package, a new set of challenges cropped up during the learning process. Not only was he determined to meet the challenge, however, but he also enjoyed the mental stimulation he experienced while teaching himself new software. Finally, Eberhard switched to using Adobe Suite 1.5, and as Adobe improved, Eberhard found it to be the most efficient design software he'd used.

FROM ARMY BUNGALOW
TO MEDIA MINISTRY

AS TECHNOLOGY INADEQUACIES have been overcome, Eberhard continues to use Adobe to create visual stories that illustrate the power of God in Africa, whether printed on paper or displayed on a digital screen. What may seem like insignificant incidents, such as encountering that 1987 computer in an unlikely time and place, in reality were chapters in God's story guiding him to TWR, where he could devote his gifts and interests to serve God's kingdom with joy. He met the woman who would become his wife, Angelika, at TWR, and they have been happily married since 1997. Angelika serves as relationship development coordinator for Africa, offering encouragement, resources and words of truth to South African listeners who reach out to the media ministry.

"Working at TWR taught me to trust God, experiencing his miracles and his workings amid the progress we are making nowadays though the use of technology," he concludes.

Father of the fatherless and protector of widows

is God in his holy habitation.

Psalm 68:5

11

The Man Who Spoke
the Word to Angola

ISAC SILVANO LOOKED warily at the large envelope.

He was in Angola, circa 2000, near the end of the 27-year civil war that had ravaged his native country.

He had been visiting an old friend in the capital city of Luanda. The friend had become a general in the armed forces. The envelope, he said, came from soldiers in the woods who were listeners to Trans World Radio, for whom Silvano produced programmes out of Swaziland (now Eswatini).

Even though the envelope came from a friend, Silvano hesitated. The use of time bombs carried in unassuming packages was common at the time in the southwestern African country.

"The security guard that was accompanying me must have sensed my hesitation, because he took the envelope and carried it to my car,"

Silvano wrote in his memoirs. "When I arrived back in the room where I was staying, I opened the envelope and found over 50 letters inside."

The letters were in response to *Yeva Ondaka* (*Listen to the Word*), the programme Silvano had prepared in his native language, Umbundu, beginning in 1976 at the invitation of Trans World Radio, while he was living in Brazil. "All were testimonies of how the messages in the programmes had impacted the listeners' hearts and minds," he wrote.

A CAREER IN RADIO

LIVING IN OBEDIENCE to God led Silvano on a path he never could have imagined for himself, a career in radio for Africa that was framed by two civil wars.

The Angolan Civil War began in 1975, shortly after the country achieved independence from Portugal, as rival factions battled for control. But Silvano, who came to faith in Jesus as a 15-year-old and was called to the ministry in 1974 while recovering from severe injuries sustained in previous military action, was in Brazil during much of the war. A church in São Paulo, Brazil, had offered to pay for his studies at a seminary in Rio de Janeiro, and the director of a shipping company arranged to get him there.

The invitation to preach the gospel to Angola came while Silvano was still in his second year of work toward his theology degree. An Angolan church initiated it in partnership with the Swiss Alliance Mission. Silvano would send the tapes of his programme to the TWR station in Swaziland, from which it would be broadcast by shortwave to Angola.

Isac Silvano recording a programme in the TWR studios in Eswatini in the late '80s.

"Letters with powerful testimonies started pouring into the station in Swaziland," Silvano wrote. "They came from all over Angola but especially from refugee camps in Zambia, Namibia and South Africa."

In time, the station in Swaziland needed Silvano to produce his own programmes. After two years of training in São Paulo, Silvano, his wife, Helena, and their two daughters moved to Swaziland in 1989 for what they thought would be a four-year stay.

That stretched to 22 years.

"This again proved that the best place to live in the world is where God sends you, no matter the challenges," Silvano wrote.

That's when Silvano's work and ministry were affected by a second civil war.

Isac Silvano shared a joyous moment with listeners of his Umbundu programme in the southern part of Angola. The photo was taken in the 2000s.

MINISTRY TO REFUGEES

MOZAMBIQUE, WHICH BORDERS Eswatini, was like Angola in that it had also been a Portuguese colony, having gained independence in 1975. Two years later, it also became embroiled in a civil war, this one lasting more than 15 years.

Many Mozambicans took refuge in Swaziland, where refugee camps were set up in Malindza and Big Bend, 40 and 70 kilometres, respectively, from the TWR site near the city of Manzini. Silvano was convicted that he needed to speak to the hearts of the refugees on Sundays, his day free from the studio. Within four weeks, he had permission to start a Bible study in each camp.

"All that need and suffering caused the refugees to seek God, and we saw several individuals give their lives to Christ every Sunday," Silvano wrote.

In less than six months, they had 50 new believers at their meetings.

A Christian man from Switzerland visited the camp and offered to send money for materials to build a church. One of the new converts had worked in construction. Soon there was a 200-seat church in each refugee camp. By the time the war ended, in October 1992, the two churches had 400 members with 10 trained leaders. With permission from authorities, the church members disassembled the buildings and brought the materials over the border. They started 10 churches in Mozambique.

ON TO ANGOLA

MEANWHILE, SILVANO WAS still producing *Yeva Ondaka*, broadcasting the programme by shortwave from Swaziland into Angola. But Angolan church leaders thought more could be done if TWR had a studio in the country. TWR chose Silvano as one of two leaders for the project. Although he never returned to his native country to live, Silvano was able to make many visits as the ministry was established. It was during one of those visits that Silvano was handed the suspicious-looking envelope that turned out to contain 50 testimonies of lives changed.

Becky Uhden, who served in the Africa Regional Office from 1993-2016, told the story in one of her prayer letters about a TWR team's visit to the administrator of a small village in the middle of Angola.

"When they greeted this important leader of the community, they were encouraged at the reception they received," Uhden wrote. "'Radio Trans Mundial – Swaziland!' he sang, imitating the very familiar voice of Isac, who stood in that very room with him. He had been listening to the broadcasts since they began in 1976!"

When their time to retire neared, Isac and Helena considered returning to Brazil, or even to Angola. But both of their daughters had moved to the United States, and the parents also ended up in Atlanta. It was not long, though, before Silvano built his own studio and continued recording programmes for Angola.

"Time has been kind to me," Silvano wrote in his memoirs. "It has given me the gift of being able to look back and see clearly the hand of God in my life and the purpose of each step over the years."

How beautiful upon the mountains
are the feet of him who brings good news,
who publishes peace,
who brings good news of happiness,
who publishes salvation,
who says to Zion, "Your God reigns."

Isaiah 52:7

12

West Africa Needs its Own Transmitting Station

B Y THE 1990S, TWR's strong transmitter in Eswatini had been on the air two decades, but the ministry still hadn't established a broadcasting station in West Africa. Broadcasts from the Eswatini station reached large portions of East and Southern Africa but were difficult to receive roughly 3 000 miles away in West Africa.

Fortunately, the SIM international missions agency operated a station in Liberia that broadcast across much of the region, and TWR partnered for many years with Radio ELWA, (Eternal Love Winning Africa). In fact, the man who today serves as TWR's international director for this region previously worked at ELWA (see the chapter featuring Abdoulaye Sangho). When war in Liberia destroyed the ELWA facilities in the 1990s, the region was left without a cross-border Christian broadcaster.

Although a land of impressive culture and continuing economic development, West Africa also struggles with serious problems: several civil wars over the years, rising religious extremism and widespread corruption, to name a few. Hundreds of people groups are still unreached by the gospel, and many missionaries will tell you that traditional animistic practices involving spells and magic exert a forbidding influence on the spiritual atmosphere. TWR leaders, including Abdoulaye Sangho, Stephen Boakye-Yiadom (then International Director of TWR Africa), and Ray Alary (then TWR Operations Director for Africa) – believed a strong Christian media presence was desperately needed in the region.

In 1998 TWR staff began seeking a country where a transmitting station could be built, but their efforts often seemed to be struggling against hostile spiritual forces. Attempts in four countries – Côte d'Ivoire, Burkina Faso, Ghana and Mali – failed to obtain a radio licence, but then a letter was received from the president of a West African country.* He had become a believer through miraculous circumstances and longed for the gospel to penetrate his country. The letter contained an invitation for TWR to build a station in his country.

It also launched the process that would bring Garth and Fiona Kennedy, the first TWR missionaries assigned to West Africa, to the region. Having remained on assignment in the region nearly 20 years as Garth led the building of the station and later the Oasis expansion project, the Kennedys are the ideal couple to recount the history of the West Africa Transmitting Station, or WATS. But they are the first to

---

*Because of security concerns, TWR chooses not to publicly disclose the location of the West Africa Transmitting Station.

point out that they were part of a team whose combined efforts were blessed by God.

"I'm very, very aware that there are a lot of people in the background that were doing a huge amount of stuff," Garth says. "We just happen to be at the tip of the spear. But I'd like to emphasize the whole team aspect and that many other people were involved on a great, great level."

BUILDING THE STATION

AS A COST engineer, one of Garth's primary responsibilities was managing construction at the transmitter site, but he and his team discovered that there were no hardware stores in the area stocking suitable materials, forcing them to create the materials by hand. In

The electrician Mathurin can be seen seated in this photo of the colorful electrical ducts being put in place before the flooring gets done.

WATS tower team in 2005. **Left to right:** Mark Blosser, Garth Kennedy, Paul Cox, Chad Creed, and Chuck Saunders.

addition to being physically demanding, the process required lots of innovative thinking. The team had to construct cement blocks to serve as bricks, and pour a huge concrete slab as the foundation for the building.

Numerous challenges faced Garth and his team of local workers and TWR staff such as James Burnett, Paul Cox, Chuck Saunders, Mark Blosser and Chad Creed to construct the building, install the technical equipment and erect the broadcast tower. Legal issues halted construction at times, and once the TWR board placed the building process on hold because the government had not granted the necessary broadcast licences.

"We had one employee or driver, and with him, we took the small bulldozer and the small backhoe, and that was when we spent three months just building the pond," Garth says. "Again, a God thing. Looking back at it, it's just phenomenal what God has done with it."

The pond has become a popular gathering place for the station staff, missionaries and expatriates in the area, and local pastors. The fish in it also are a valuable protein source for station workers and their families.

Finally, the day projected for the broadcasting launch was drawing near. But leading up to it was a stretch of several long days, often working well into the night, to solve technical problems.

And then it happened: The transmitters finally turned on that morning, triggering an eruption of praise. The uproar spread like wildfire as thankfulness overflowed from the crew's hearts.

Garth was outside in the garage when technicians darted out of the building and toward the vehicle. Worship music blared forth as they switched on the wind-up radio in the car. As the music swelled, it couldn't outgrow the joy rising inside each team member's heart. Tears welled up in many of the missionaries' eyes, including Fiona's.

When the official planned launch day arrived on Feb. 1, 2008, programming went out over the airwaves to West Africa, bringing the gospel in multiple languages through AM radio.

GOD'S GUIDING HAND AMID SPIRITUAL WARFARE

GARTH AND FIONA are from South Africa, though Fiona was born in northern Zambia. They graduated from the University of Witwatersrand in Johannesburg, Garth studying cost engineering and Fiona receiving a medical degree. Both feeling God's call to missions, they first served with another ministry in Egypt before learning about TWR and being asked to help start the work in West Africa.

Initially planning to oversee the building of WATS and remain there 18 months, their tenure in the country has stretched to nearly two decades. The Kennedys' sons, Daniel and Timothy, have spent most of their lives there and clearly consider it to be home. Despite the roots put down by the family and their faithful commitment to the area and the work, however, Garth acknowledges that the setbacks and discouragement that sometimes experienced were "huge, absolutely huge."

In fact, Garth recalls, he was once so discouraged that he told Fiona he was ready to quit the job and leave the country. There was one problem, though: In this time before easy payment methods and online air reservations, they didn't have the cash to visit a travel agent and buy tickets for the family.

"I think God ordained that we had no cash," he says. "... We had some real discouragements, but I look back at that, and it's just incredible how God built us through those times and the setbacks we had."

Another source of discouragement was the spiritual oppression resulting from traditional occultic practices. Fetishes, made from animal carcasses and intended as a spell or curse, were placed at the station gate and a door, stirring fear among some local workers. Another time, one of these workers became deathly afraid and accused a co-worker of casting a spell on him. Garth's efforts to mediate between the two Christian men and mend their relationship were unsuccessful, despite no evidence suggesting that the accused had acted intentionally wrong. Regrettably, the accuser had to be dismissed.

The transmitter building a couple of days prior to the dedication in 2008 with one medium wave antenna tower seen behind it.

WATS EXPANDS TO MEET DEMAND

AS THE KENNEDYS' initial 18 months at WATS grew into a decade plus, audience needs were also growing. Demands for more programming were on the rise from Nigeria, which is Africa's most-populated country and splintered between the mostly Muslim north and mostly Christian south. This nation of 218 million people has been called the most dangerous place in the world to be a Christian.

Bible broadcasts are badly needed in both halves of the country, of course, but WATS' single transmitter schedule was already full. The decision was made to install another AM transmitter to handle the broadcasting to Nigeria and its immediate surrounding area while the first transmitter would focus on other parts of the region. The second transmitter would be dubbed Oasis, symbolizing the living water that it would deliver to Nigeria.

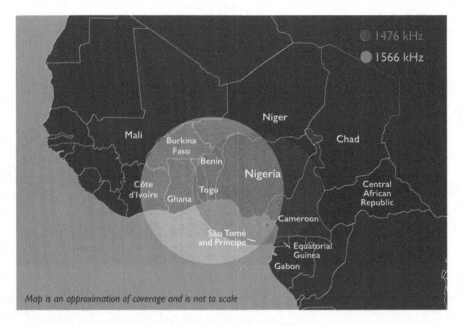

This map shows the broadcast coverage of the two West Africa medium wave transmitters. The 1476 Khz transmitter is known as Oasis.

With TWR International leading the fundraising, and national partner TWR Canada especially keen to be involved, over 4 800 supporters gave more than $1.45 million to make the Oasis project possible. Telecommunications company Swisscom donated a decommissioned AM transmitter that could operate at 150 000 watts, and unpacking it and getting all the sensitive electronics working again required lots of specialized effort.

Technical contractors, volunteers, TWR staff members and even some former staff members visited WATS to assist with the installation. Paul Cox, who played a key role in the initial establishment of the transmitting station, along with Dick Veldman, Graham Kimber, Perry Beabout and many others, travelled to the site to help Garth and the WATS team bring Oasis to life. All the efforts bore fruit when the Oasis officially took to the airwaves on Feb. 1, 2020, just as the COVID-19 pandemic was emerging. The reception in Nigeria has been extremely encouraging, judging not only from the amount of listener feedback but also from queries and complaints sent via WhatsApp by disappointed audience members when rare technical glitches keep Oasis off the air.

Garth said a TWR ministry partner, whose name remains undisclosed as a security precaution, "is a real dear brother in Christ … who has done a phenomenal job in Nigeria, traveling around, sharing about the ministry, handing out radios. It's very difficult for him, but he has been phenomenal."

Today, Oasis broadcasts biblical programming in six languages to Nigeria. Messages via phone, email and social media provide evidence that the outreach is making an impact.

"I really appreciate your programme, sir. The Lord will strengthen the ministry. Continue to pray for us in the north. We are facing terrible persecutions here."

"I [belong to another religion], but I cannot afford to miss your programme because it is encouraging, and I believe what you are saying is from God."

"I [belong to another religion]. For now, I do not want to reveal my identity. I want to become a Christian. When the time comes, I will call back to you without hiding my number. Please pray for me."

And God is able to make all grace abound to you,
so that having all sufficiency in all things at all
times, you may abound in every good work.

2 Corinthians 9:8

13

God Uses Technology (and Technicians) for Missions

THE LORD DELIGHTS in using willing hearts to spread the gospel, and whatever skill set a believer has, the Lord can use it for his name's sake.

With a gift for problem-solving and understanding computers, Gottfried Schiele's story exemplifies the truth as explained in Ephesians 2:10. "For we are his workmanship," Paul tells us, "created in Christ Jesus for good works, which God prepared beforehand, that we should walk in them." God desires to use believers like Gottfried as evidence of his divine workmanship.

Gottfried Schiele working in his office in Manzini, Eswatini, in the early '90s.

A DESIRE TO SERVE

A DESIRE LINGERED deep in Gottfried's heart. It was a desire that produced a vague vision, as if someone had smeared a wet portrait, the outline of a face discernible but the precise identity still blurry. What exactly did God have in store for him?

He wanted to enter ministry or missions in one form or another. From the perspective of the average observer, Gottfried's skills seemed to lie outside the realm of missions, but the wisdom of God is different from the wisdom of man.

Working in a veterinary lab in a vaccine factory, Gottfried engaged with computers daily, shifting from the kind of tasks most people would envision in a laboratory setting to the highly technical activities involved in running computers. In the 1980s, Gottfried not only witnessed the computerisation of his Pretoria, South Africa, factory but also aided the process.

As the call to serve in ministry strengthened, a clearer idea seemed to take shape. Rather than shepherding a computer system, perhaps God was calling him to become a pastor and shepherd a body of believers. In light of this vision, he started university study in Greek and theology in addition to his work at Onderstepoort Vaccine Factory. But hurdles emerged, and he realised that pastoring might not be what he was called to do in ministry.

"I realised that academic-level-type studies in ministry, pastorate, whatever it may be was not my thing," says Gottfried.

Despite the trials, he wasn't deterred from seeking another way to serve. It was as if he'd rolled a giant stone down a steep hill, and nothing could break the momentum. Nothing could quench his eagerness to serve the Lord.

GOTTFRIED FINDS TWR

AT EACH OPPORTUNITY, though, he felt the door slam shut. Each slam brought discouragement, but he kept seeking new doors to knock on. Determined to use his time wisely as he searched, Gottfried connected with TWR South Africa as a volunteer and then decided perhaps the media ministry was the answer to his call to Christian service.

"I didn't want to just sit around doing nothing, so I volunteered time, and I spoke with the director at that point," Gottfried says. "He said that the South Africa office didn't have anything, but he said he would look around."

The director in South Africa contacted the director of TWR's transmitting station in Eswatini (then known as Swaziland). It just so happened that the Eswatini director had been thinking about creating a new position, though he was still rounding out the details of the role. The role, however, would definitely involve computers.

Hope glimmered inside Gottfried. Perhaps the time in the vaccine factory was prepping him for this. Perhaps his interest in computers would translate into ministry. His interest was a God-given gift that brought him enjoyment, but perhaps he could also use it for the gospel.

After a meeting with the Eswatini director, he was offered the new position. By the time he left the vaccine factory in 1992, he had experience working on a company network connected to about 500 PCs.

When October rolled by, Gottfried moved to Eswatini to work in what was then TWR's Africa Regional Office in Manzini, officially beginning full-time Christian service as a computer specialist. Well-acquainted with the process of computerising a large organization, Gottfried helped pull electrical cables, acquired the necessary materials and installed equipment. The office started with an IBM server, terminals, and a modem for emails. For communications, there were phone lines, fax, and telex, and snail mail.

Two and a half years later, he moved to the United States to work in the Cary, North Carolina, office, then returned to Pretoria, where he served until the new facility nearby Kempton Park was built and became TWR Africa's regional office.

THE TWR AFRICA OFFICE EXPANDS

IN KEMPTON PARK, he witnessed the Lord blessing TWR Africa. From other office locations, staff members came. New staff members joined, and the TWR Africa ministry flourished. More Africans across the continent were hearing the gospel and accepting Christ.

As the office expanded, so did use of the internet along with an accompanying problem.

Gottfried Schiele working on network cables at the Africa Regional Office in Kempton Park in that late 2000s.

In the late 2000s, the TWR office expanded beyond its network switch, which is a piece of equipment that enables computers to communicate with one another. While almost 300 ports were needed for the office, only 96 ports were available. Also, the switch acted like a temperamental child – obedient some days and defiant on others.

"We were growing at quite a tremendous rate and had more computers and more devices that needed to be connected up," says Gottfried. "The old switches were very finicky. One day, they would work fine, and the next day they wouldn't work the same way we needed them to."

When staff often encountered internet problems on the job, they had to leave their office spaces and knock on Gottfried's door to ask for help. Gottfried and the IT team had to abandon their work temporarily to investigate and solve the issues.

As the problem worsened, a clear realisation settled inside Gottfried and the TWR office. They needed an upgrade. Costs were calculated, but a new switch didn't fit into the budget. Knowing that the Lord would provide whatever was required, the team laid their need at his feet in prayer during devotions and staff meetings.

GOD MOVES A HEART TO GIVE

GOTTFRIED NEVER FIGURED out how the donor discovered that the office needed a network switch.

The donor was already active in a ministry that spoke hope to prisoners, and when he found out about the need, he immediately expressed his desire to help TWR.

"I want to send you this device. Tell me where I can get it, how much it's going to cost, and I'll have it sent to you," he said.

One of the donor's children worked in the computer industry and found a Cisco core switch with an abundance of units that would provide extensive networking capabilities. It also possessed two power supplies. If one power supply crashed, the other would operate instead. Not only would it be a reliable switch, but its technological capacity could also carry the office's needs. Their new telephone system would no longer need an extra power supply, but they could connect it to the switch to receive its power directly from it.

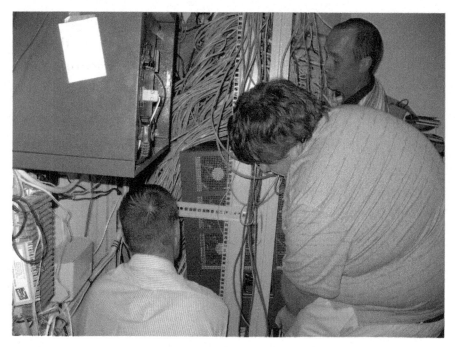

Gottfried Schiele, Bud Driver and Mike Edmundson installing the new network switch into a rack where it will be conected to the various network cables.

Not only did the donor locate the device, but God placed it on his heart to provide the funds. For almost 15 years, the network switch met the needs of the expanding ministry, and even after its time, God provided yet another one that kept pace with the office's growth so his work in Africa continued to be done.

A TESTIMONY OF GOD'S CHARACTER

PLAYING A SIGNIFICANT role in TWR's technological growth, Gottfried continues to implement network, internet, and playout upgrades to keep TWR abreast of rapid technology advancement. As guardians behind the scenes, Gottfried and the team have defended and protected the TWR Africa ministry from malicious software, cyberattacks and data breaches that would endanger TWR's security.

It's easy to see why Gottfried views TWR as an unambiguous testimony of God's provision, for he has witnessed that provision abundantly in the realm of technology. These advanced tools enable TWR to reach out to huge numbers of people in geographically, politically, economically or culturally isolated areas, and God, often through a generous band of supporters, has provided every step of the way.

To Gottfried, it's supremely encouraging that an all-knowing, all-powerful God faithfully ensures that the ministry's technology needs are met in his own perfect way and timing.

You will receive power when the Holy Spirit has come upon you, and you will be my witnesses in Jerusalem and in all Judea and Samaria, and to the end of the earth.

Acts 1:8

14

Spreading God's Word to Radio Hobbyists

ALTHOUGH SHE SERVES in Africa with TWR, Lorraine Stavropoulos' love for people who haven't met Jesus Christ stretches far beyond this continent and across the oceans. Like the long roots of a mighty oak, Lorraine's singular ministry connects with people living in many countries around the globe, from Japan to Italy, Brazil to Indonesia, and China to the Middle East.

As TWR Africa's DX secretary, Lorraine reaches them through DXing,* a hobby in which radio enthusiasts strive to tune in and identify signals from distant stations, often hundreds or even thousands of miles away. Many DXers then get in touch with the distant stations whose signals they receive, offer a brief report of what, where, when

---

*DX comes from the telegraphic abbreviation for "distance."

and how the signal was heard, and ask for QSL* cards, which are simple acknowledgements that the report was received.

DXers collect these cards like trophies showing how many far-flung frequencies they've tuned in. And it's these cards that Lorraine recognized as a creative way to plant gospel seeds. To stir DXers' interest in the gospel, she ensures that each response is prayed over and personalised, whether through a Bible verse or a photograph chosen to embellish the QSL card.

DIGITAL RUSHES PAST SNAIL MAIL

BORN IN BOKSBURG, South Africa, Lorraine joined TWR when she married Steve Stavropoulos, who was already serving as an engineer with the ministry. They married in January 1979, and two weeks after their honeymoon, they moved to Eswatini (formerly known as Swaziland) as a missionary couple.

Only a couple of years after joining TWR, Lorraine got involved with responding to QSL requests. She sent the cards via snail mail to DXers who reported their reception of the Eswatini transmitter's broadcasts, including to hobbyists outside Africa.

Devoted to sharing the gospel, she finds creative tactics to spur DXers' interest in the Bible, but when she first started serving, many of the gospel-sharing strategies she now uses hadn't been adopted. Through changing technology and God-given foresight, she used her

---

QSL is an international code effectively confirming receipt of a transmission.

An example of a QSL card sent to DXers in 1975. The back of the card contained the details of the person requesting proof that they had found a new shortwave radio station.

wisdom and passion for the gospel to create the changes God put on her heart.

The QSL cards used to be handwritten and printed, each card identical regardless of what country they were sent to, and about 1 000 were printed at a time. It was the cheapest way to produce and send the cards.

"Being a junior, I could not have a say in what was on it. In fact, for years we used the same QSL," says Lorraine.

God kindled in Lorraine's heart a desire to communicate with DXers in a way that takes into account their interests, culture and spiritual state, and God paved a path for Lorraine to do so.

As technology progressed, Lorraine saw the opportunity to move away from snail mail. Instead, QSL cards would be sent through email, and Lorraine helped in the transition to e-cards. The transition to e-cards allowed for greater customisation of the QSL responses in an effort to meet the diverse needs of the recipients.

GOD PROVIDES CREATIVITY AND INSIGHT

LORRAINE QUICKLY TAUGHT herself how to create and send e-cards. Catering to the DXers' fascination with radio technology, she began acquiring photos showcasing the station's uncommon equipment to decorate the e-cards.

Although ministry to the Japanese was considered very difficult, Japanese listeners were connecting to the TWR Eswatini frequencies by the hundreds. QSL card requests letters came in from countries where English wasn't the native language, including Japan, 8 000 miles away and widely known as having the world's second-largest unreached population. Lorraine's heart burned to share the Scriptures with DXers in their heart language rather than in English.

It was the start of something big, and soon DXers around the world were receiving English QSL cards containing Bible verses in their own heart languages.

God put a desire in Lorraine's heart to share specific verses with DXers. She wanted them to recognize the temporary, passing nature of the world and then to focus on death and the afterlife.

"My aim, with the help of the Lord, is to make people think about eternity," she says.

Now able to customize messages QSL cards, she began to incorporate references to other biblical resources, including the abundant Christian content on twr360.org, further exposing recipients to God's Word. She overflows with thankfulness that digital QSL cards came to replace the snail-mail version.

This is to verify that
heard us on 21st August, 2024, on 7410 kHz
At 18:20-19:001UTC www.twr360.org *Lorraine Stavropoulos*

twr
Speaking Hope to the World

[7] The LORD keeps you from all harm and watches over your life. [8] The LORD keeps watch over you as you come and go, both now and forever. Psalms 121:7-8

An example of a QSL card that was created in response to a request from a DXer, in 2024. This card was sent via email. The photo in this card is an aerial view of the transmitter building.

"With the advent of digital things, I could generate them individually," she says. "Some people send many requests for QSL cards. Every time I answer them, I use a different Bible verse."

As she continues serving in the DX ministry, Lorraine cultivates and treasures maintaining a prayerful spirit. She's keenly aware that the cards go out to individuals from various walks of life and cultures. Only God knows what will seize their attentions and move their hearts, so as she prepares each QSL card, she prays for guidance to determine which Scripture passage, photo and resource recommendations to incorporate on the card.

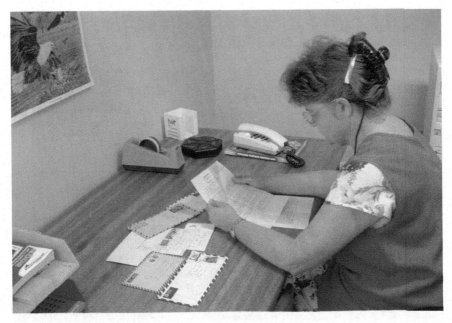

Lorraine Stavropolous reading listener letters that had been sent to the TWR Manzini office in the '90s.

GLOBAL IMPACT VIA AFRICAN MINISTRY

A THOUSAND STORIES cluster behind why people pursue DXing, but the Lord has given Lorraine a deep desire to reach them. Through the ministry, some DXers have even reached out to Lorraine, asking for help and seeking answers.

Though she can't keep track of which ones simply keep the cards as a trophy of their hobby versus those whom the cards have affected spiritually, Lorraine experiences a deep peace and joy in the task. She knows that the power of God will work through the cards in the way he sees fit and that her role is to obey the calling as his faithful servant. Isaiah 55:11 encourages her:

> *"So shall my word be that goes out from my mouth; it shall not return to me empty, but it shall accomplish that which I purpose, and shall succeed in the thing for which I sent it."*

God and his Word have the power to change lives, Lorraine understands, so she directs DXers to Scripture and continually praises him for using her to reach out to the lost while providing for the Stavropouloses through each step of their missionary service.

Do not lay up for yourselves treasures on earth,
where moth and rust destroy and where thieves break
in and steal, but lay up for yourselves treasures in
heaven, where neither moth nor rust destroys and
where thieves do not break in and steal. For where
your treasure is, there your heart will be also.

Matthew 6:19-21

15

A Treasure Never
Lost or Decayed

WHAT DO YOU think of when you hear the word "treasure"?

Perhaps you think of a giant chest with iron locks, ancient and rusted shut, but within, that chest cradles forgotten pirate treasure from centuries before, rich with history and vanished times.

Perhaps you think of a jewellery box with diamond necklaces locked inside. Like glittering vines, the necklace strands tumble out the moment you open it, and the gems reflect iridescent shapes across the walls, momentarily blinding your eyes.

But treasure comes in all shapes and sizes, and there is a treasure worth immeasurably more than sparkling gems.

Tobi Pfeiffer working at his work station at the Eswatini transmitter site.

TREASURES CONTAINED IN MODERN CONTAINERS

NOW, IMAGINE A small rectangular piece of plastic topped by metal. It's flat, about the size of a thumb. Within, a treasure of boundless price is obscured. It contains no forgotten gold or diamonds. Rather, it holds the powerful Word of the Lord voiced and sung in a multitude of languages.

And this Word has the power to save and transform.

Tucked in envelopes, the small rectangular pieces of plastic – USB drives – were the bearers of the treasure, shipped from Kempton Park, South Africa, to the TWR transmitter site in Eswatini more than 400 kilometres away. Over the South African roads, surrounded by tree farms and brown mountains, and along the roads of Eswatini, rippling with hills painted in strokes of leafy green, the envelopes were delivered every week.

Since joining TWR in 2009, Tobi Pfeiffer had worked with the technical team to receive and tear open those envelopes at the Eswatini transmitter site. From the USB drives, they uploaded the radio programmes in the playout system that would broadcast gospel hope to the people of southern and eastern Africa.

And Tobi always saw the USB drives arrive safely. He never experienced a lost programme.

Not only were they never lost. There was always a chance that the audio on the drives could be corrupted. For example, a power surge or even humidity could affect the digital data and garble the audio. If corrupted, the programmes couldn't be modified. Rather, the corruption would stain the programme like

Above: 12-inch reels playing content for broadcasts. The smaller reel contains continuity and announcements.

Below: USB memory sticks like these were used at the Eswatini transmitter site. In 2008, one of these contained about one week's worth of content. By 2014, they contained roughly 16 weeks' worth, and currently, in 2024, all content is sent via the internet.

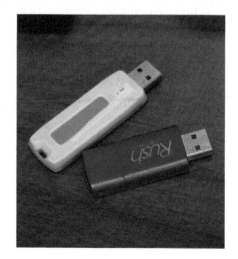

permanent ink. Yet during his time, Tobi saw the Lord provide, for he rarely received a corrupted drive.

HOWEVER SENT, THE TREASURE WAS HOPE

ONLY A COUPLE of years after Tobi started, the USB drives stopped coming in the mail. It wasn't because they went missing; instead, the programmes began to be transported over the internet. Rather than trekking the African roads, the data traversed the pathway of the internet or even travelled by satellite, allowing Tobi and the staff to achieve further efficiency.

Despite the shift to a more efficient technology, Tobi firmly attests that the listener experience never changed. The listeners still received the daily encouragement they anticipated via the gospel broadcasts, finding hope amidst the challenges they face.

Whether transported in a bolted chest, on a rectangular piece of plastic or over the passageways of the internet, the treasure of God's Word is never intended to remain confined. It is most valuable when spread far and wide through the protection and faithfulness of the Lord, unchanging in his desire for the lost to know him.

Two are better than one, because they have a good reward for their toil. For if they fall, one will lift up his fellow. But woe to him who is alone when he falls and has not another to lift him up!

Ecclesiastes 4:9-12

16

God's Power Against the Storm

GOD CULTIVATED THE transmitter site in Eswatini, then known as Swaziland, so that it produced abundant fruit in the decades following its establishment. But storms sometimes swept in, seemingly threatening to destroy the fruit.

Nothing overpowers the gospel, however. As the apostle Paul declares in 2 Timothy, "Wherein I suffer trouble, as an evil doer, even unto bonds; but the Word of God is not bound."

The gospel calms the storms whipped up by Satan. Salema Simelane, a senior technician for 20 years at the Eswatini site, has witnessed the power of God Almighty to withstand both metaphorical and literal storms when they imperiled the gospel-broadcasting station.

Salema Simelane and Sicelo Dlamini repairing a part of a shortwave antenna.

A WILLING HEART

WHEN SALEMA'S CELL-PHONE rang that April morning in 2015, he wasn't prepared for the emergency that was about to interrupt his holiday week and send him rushing back to the TWR transmitter site where he worked.

Like many of his Eswatini compatriots, he had the week off in celebration of the birthday of his country's king, Mswati III. Salema and his wife and three children were spending the break catching up on the cultivation of their wheat crop.

The 8 am phone call broke into those plans and soon would have him making the two-hour drive back to the Eswatini Transmitter Site (ESWATS). One of his bosses was on the other end of the line with bad news for the technician.

The day before, a heavy storm had swept through the small, landlocked country and struck the area around ESWATS particularly hard. While rain came down in torrents, winds cut a swath through the transmitter site, felling trees and wreaking havoc. The alliance of wind and rain took down most of the site's feed lines, including the poles. A feed line is a cable that "feeds" the signal from the transmitter to the antenna, from which the signal goes out to radios across southern Africa.

For a broadcaster whose primary purpose is to bring God's Word to as many hearts and homes as possible, this was nearly as bad as it gets: The disrupted signals left countless listeners unable to tune into their radio programmes.

Frustration could have boiled inside Salema. A trace of bitterness could have started to spread. He was called to leave his family, plans, and holiday and to travel two hours to the transmitter site, where strategizing and performing repair and manual effort waited. But rather than annoyance churning inside him, an overwhelming sense of excitement welled up.

"When we received the call, we drove right away to Manzini to give a hand to help the other engineers to fix the feed lines, because I really like my job, and I'm called to do this job," Salema says. "So, I was so happy to be part of the team to repair the feed lines and the antennas."

THE DESTRUCTION

GATHERING HIS THINGS, Salema acted as fast as possible, thrilled to be a part of the process of repairing the site. He left his home, situated on the south side of Eswatini near the South African border, to drive to the transmitter's location. A sense of peace and trust in the Lord followed him because he knew that God would use him in the repair process.

The storm caused several feed line poles to bend and fall over. These particular feed lines take the signal from the transmitters to one of the short wave antennas.

A senior technician, Salema knew his skills would be needed, for his day-to-day activities often involved what would be needed in this emergency: ensuring that the transmitters were working properly, climbing towers and repairing broken machinery.

When Salema arrived at the site, he spotted the obvious destruction, which seemed to spell out in large letters that the job would not be easy. The feed lines stretched out from the transmitter building side in rows, but most of the poles were down. Lines hung down, creating a chaos of metal and wire. Two of the feed lines were completely down, while the others were contorted and humped in disarray.

Salema and the team assessed their available skills and manpower and quickly realized that they didn't have enough hands to fix the downed lines and limp antennas and get gospel programmes back on the air without delay.

GOD'S PROVISION, PIECE BY PIECE

DESPITE THE ABSENCE of resources, God's hand moved through the entire crisis, and Salema witnessed it moment by moment, day by day.

Since they couldn't restore the feed lines and poles without proper equipment, the team searched for a company that owned the machinery needed to mend the damage. With God's help, they contacted an electric company based in Manzini that was willing to come and work, despite it being the holidays.

But God had another plan to provide.

When the storm hit, several experienced and technically knowledgeable TWR missionaries happened to be visiting in Johannesburg. Receiving the call for help, Steve and Lorraine Stavropoulos, James Burnett and Mark Blosser gladly dropped their plans and drove to Eswatini to join the effort.

In addition to witnessing God's provision of staff, Salema witnessed the love found in the family of Christ as believers came alongside engineers and staff in encouragement and prayer. The missionary families pitched in with their presence, care, prayer and encouragement. Salema remembers the warmth Britta Pfeiffer and her sons brought when they visited the site. Britta and the other missionaries planned

With the help of the electrical company, the team at the transmitter site is able to repair fallen-over feed line poles.

the baking, snacks and drinks that were shared on the site. Everyone held a commitment in their hearts as believers, while staff and supporters across the globe supported the team through prayer.

As the team worked out the logistics and used temporary guide ropes to pull the poles up, thoughts of listeners who would be missing the Bible broadcasts weighed on Salema's mind. The importance of those listeners hearing God's Word tugged at his heart and drove him to do whatever was necessary to mend the feedlines and antennas.

BROADCASTING AGAIN

EARLY ON, THE staff experienced a huge blessing and fervently thanked the Lord for it. As a temporary solution, they were able to use undamaged antennas to get programmes back on the air. Though it took two weeks to fully repair the damaged facilities, only a small amount of the broadcast time was interrupted.

To this day, Salema testifies that the Lord provided the Eswatini site with his help and protection when an actual storm arose and threatened to cut off gospel broadcasts. He finds fulfillment not only in serving the Lord by overcoming technical challenges but also in knowing that his work helps bring believers and seekers closer to God.

"We are really enjoying our work, and we are always making sure the transmitters are always on air," he says. "Listeners can't listen to programmes without us. We really thank God. He gave us the opportunity to contribute in spreading the good news to the whole world."

He established a testimony in Jacob
and appointed a law in Israel,
which he commanded our fathers
to teach to their children,
that the next generation might know them,
the children yet unborn,
and arise and tell them to their children,
so that they should set their hope in God
and not forget the works of God,
but keep his commandments.

Psalm 78:5-7

Epilogue

TWR AFRICA LOOKS TO THE NEXT GENERATION

AS TWR AFRICA celebrates what God has done through the first 50 years of this ministry, its leaders are preparing for how TWR will be used for a new generation.

"If the founder, Paul Freed, started now, he would try to reach the people of today, not the people of yesterday," said Abdoulaye Sangho, international director for West and Central Africa.

As Africans more and more turn to smartphones and social media for their information and entertainment, TWR is adapting to the digital world, Sangho said. "TWR needs to be there for the next generation. If we want to reach the next generation, that's where we should go."

Victor Kaonga - photo taken during a visit to the TWR Africa offices in Kempton Park.

Victor Kaonga, international director for East and Southern Africa, agreed.

"We do have several opportunities, which are exciting, some are emerging now," he said. "Especially when it comes to using digital platforms to reach mostly, I'd say, the younger generation."

One new wave that is starting to be used in parts of the region is "visual radio," Kaonga said. While listeners hear a programme on an FM station, they can also watch the presenter online. Visual radio already is being used in Malawi, Zambia and Kenya, he said.

"Young people love that mix," Kaonga said. "They can [capture] the audiences that were being lost by the very fact that we're limiting ourselves to audio only."

The programme formats also will continue to change, he said.

"I'm seeing the desire for more, I would say, journalistic productions," Kaonga said. "TWR traditionally runs lots of long sermon-based programmes, but I think that is really changing."

He cited *Worship ConneXion*, a weekday afternoon programme broadcast by TWR Africa stations and on satellite radio by New Life Africa, as an example of programming appealing to a younger audience.

This particularly matters in Africa, which has the 20 youngest countries – in terms of median age – in the world, according to the CIA World Factbook*. In Angola, for example, the median age is 16.3; in Uganda it's 16.2; and in Niger it's 15.2.

TWR Africa is responding to the challenge, in part, with talented, knowledgeable and godly young leaders. Janet Mtali, national director of TWR

Janet Mtali during an interview at TWR's national headquarters in Cary, USA.

Malawi for more than a year, is 34. That puts her in line with the population of her country, 75% of whom are younger than 35. Mtali started her TWR Malawi career by doing programmes for kids while she was still in high school.

She wants to make sure TWR Malawi is continuing to connect with younger listeners.

"We've done recruitment specifically for a producer for young people," Mtali said. "And we're trying to be more intentional with that."

---

*This information is according to the most recently updated information from the CIA Factbook (https://www.cia.gov/the-world-factbook/) at the time GOLDEN was pulished.

As new formats and new platforms are developed, radio – including shortwave and medium wave – remains a vital part of the work of TWR Africa.

"There is still a place for radio because in many places there is no possibility for electricity or power," Sangho said.

Kaonga noted that radio is still an invaluable tool in regions with high rates of illiteracy. It's also a tool for reaching closed countries.

When countries increase restrictions on broadcast and internet access, TWR is able to "enter" those countries with the good news of Jesus through broadcasts from outside the countries, he explained. He quickly named four countries in East and Southern Africa where that is occurring.

So even as the number of listeners for the older forms of media seem to dwindle, there may continue to be a place for the range offered by shortwave and medium-wave broadcasting.

"On the one end, we are kind of stretched, we are afraid that we may lose on the audiences for shortwave and medium wave," Kaonga said. "But somehow, this might be the saving moment. This same shortwave media might be the saviour."

The Golden Thread of Time

1954

TWR starts broadcasting the gospel as Voice of Tangier.

1959

Gospel broadcaster ERF in Germany is founded, initiating our national partnership model, which continues to this day.

1971

1973

Larry and Virginia McGuire land in South Africa to serve as missionaries.

TWR purchases the Mpangela Ranch in Eswatini.

1974  1974

1974

TWR starts their first regular broadcasts from Eswatini to Africa.

Evert and Edie Kleynhans receives a call from TWR to "temporarily" serve with TWR to assist in the building of the Eswatini transmitter site. They stay for 17 years.

A significant storm sweeps through Eswatini causing sand, suitable for building, to wash up on the banks of the river running through Mpangela Ranch.

1975

Stephen Boakye-Yiadom joins ERF as an intern.

1975

TWR receives 3323 letters in response to programming aired from the transmitting station in Eswatini.

1976

Stephen Boakye-Yiadom moves to Nairobi, Kenya to lead a TWR Office.

TWR Kenya, TWR's first partner in Africa is established.

Isac Silvano starts producing *Yeva Ondaka* (Listen to the Word) in his native language of Umbundu at the invitation of TWR, while living in Brazil.

1977

A curtain wave antenna for short-wave (SW) is set up in Eswatini.

1978

Steve Stavropoulos moves to the Eswatini transmitter site as a full-time missionary with TWR.

Andrew and Barbara MacDonald join TWR, serving remotely from their home in Cape Town, South Africa.

1979

Steve and Lorraine Stavropoulos get married and Lorraine starts serving alongside her husband in various roles.

TWR receives a license to broadcast using medium wave (MW) from Eswatini.

1981

TWR starts broadcasting using MW, on frequency 1170 kHz, from Eswatini into Southern Africa.

1982

TWR builds a shortwave transmitting station, which was known as Radio 540, in Bophuthatswana, now part of South Africa. Later that year the station goes on air.

James Burnett joins TWR as a shift engineer at the transmitter site.

1984

Tropical Storm Domoina sweeps across Eswatini causing the access bridge to the transmitter site to be unusable.

1984

Staff had to carry heavy steel boxes across the narrow swing bridge while the road was unusable.

1987

The World Wide Web (www.) is developed, launching the Internet into a new era of international internet usage.

1987

Lyn Burnett starts recording announcements that would be played in between regular gospel programmes broadcast over SW and MW.

1990

Eberhard Haberkorn joins TWR South Africa as a studio technician.

1989

Isac Silvano and his family move to Eswatini and as part of his ministry he starts Bible study groups in Mozambican refugee camps that were relatively close to Manzini, Eswatni. These Bible study groups grow into churches.

1992

Andrew MacDonald is asked to open the Africa Regional Office (ARO) in Kempton Park, South Africa.

Stephen Boakye-Yiadom becomes the International Director for TWR Africa and moves to South Africa with his wife and four children.

Gottfried Schiele begins his missionary service with TWR in Eswatini.

After the Mozambican civil war ends, ten churches are started in seven different provinces as a result of Isac Silvano's ministry.

1993

Becky Uhden relocates to South Africa to assist with setting up the Finance Department for the Africa Regional Office..

1995

Andrew MacDonald steps down from his position as a ministry director for Africa and serves as a consultant.

Eberhard Haberkorn adds graphic design to his growing list of skills and works on the layout of newsletters.

1996

TWR Africa starts using satellite to air broadcasts in English, French and Swahili.

Rev. Abdoulaye Sangho renovates a child's bedroom to begin recording *Africa Challenge* in French. Later this year he accepts an invitation to join the TWR Africa ministry.

1996

twr.org debuts on the internet.

1998

TWR Africa begins looking for a good location to build a transmitter site in West Africa.

1999

The Swazi king, King Mswati III, attends TWR Africa's 25th anniversary celebration at the transmitter site.

1999

Gottfried Schiele uses his musical gift of playing English Handbells at TWR Africa's 25th anniversary celebration.

2000

Eberhard starts using Abobe InDesign which he uses to this day, although the features have drastically advanced.

2001

TWR Africa launches twrafrica.org.

TWR Africa builds their new ARO building in Kempton Park.

2002

Garth and Fiona Kennedy join TWR as missionaries.

TWR sets up an office in Côte d'Ivoire for ministry in West and Central Africa. This region is often referred to as WeCAf.

2003

The Africa Traffic System (ATS) software system, developed by Gottfried Schiele, is installed at ARO and Swaziland.

2004

TWR is given the green light to build a MW transmitter site in a West African country.

2007

Stephen Boakye-Yiadom passes away.

TWR Africa starts to stream their 24/7 radio station on their website.

2009

Tobi Pfeifer and his wife, Britta, join TWR.

TWR Africa publishes a book about the story behind the establishment of TWR's West African transmitter site.

2007

The iPhone is released, starting the rapid adoption of the smart phone as an important medium for not only communication but also using the internet on the go and changing the way people use social media.

2008

The first transmitter at the West African transmitter site (WATS) goes on air on frequency 1566 kHz.

2011

Isac Silvano retires and moves to Atlanta, USA, with his wife, where he continues recording programmes for Angola.

2012

ARO expands their building to include a lodge and extra offices dubbed "West Wing."

2013

The online portal TWR360 launches with access to on-demand biblical content in multiple languages.

2014

Rev. Abdoulaye Sangho becomes the international director for the ministry in West and Cental Africa.

2015

A major storm sweeps through Eswatini causing severe damage to feedlines and antennas at the transmitter site.

Several experienced engineers including Steve Stavropoulos and James Burnett travel from South Africa to Eswatini to assist with repairs of the damages caused by the storm.

2018

In April the Kingdom of Swaziland is renamed to the Kingdom of Eswatini as it is commonly used in the Swazi language.

2020

WATS receives a licence for a second MW transmitter on 1476 kHz. This transmitter, (dubbed OASIS), goes on air, bringing the living water of Jesus to spiritually dry and barren land of Nigeria and surrounding countries.

2022

Open AI releases ChatGPT which has started a new era of how we interact with information and technology.

2024

TWR is awarded the 'Faith Counts Award' from the Faith Broadcasting Network at the 2024 Association of Christian Media conference in recognition of a series of 15-minute Zulu audio programmes called *Sakha Indoda* (Building a Man).

About the Authors

HANNAH DAVIS

Hannah Davis is a writer from Cary, North Carolina. Her passion for writing sparked as a child when she began writing fictional novels in her spare time. Her passion led her to earn her BA in English Rhetoric and Professional Writing from North Carolina State University. Her work has been featured in *Christianity Today Magazine*. To contribute to **GOLDEN:** *TWR's 50-year journey of bringing Jesus to Africa*, she travelled to South Africa and spent the summer interviewing and writing at TWR's South Africa office. When she isn't writing, she can be found walking in nature, traveling, or enjoying a good cappuccino. Her favourite Bible verse is Ephesians 2:10.

JOHN LUNDY

A native of Estherville, Iowa, John Lundy came to faith in Christ as a young boy and experienced a deepening personal relationship with Jesus through fellow students at the University of Missouri-Columbia and through a church in Michigan City, Indiana. He has a bachelor's degree in journalism from Missouri and had a 40-year newspaper career in Indiana, Ohio and Duluth, Minnesota. Sensing a call to a late-career missions assignment, he connected with TWR. After 13 months of raising a ministry partnership team, he came to TWR in January 2022 as a writer and editor in the Cary, North Carolina, office. He's single and lives in lives in Cary, North Carolina.

Made in the USA
Columbia, SC
05 March 2025

54709747R00089